Lessons in Organisin

'An excellent review of the attack on teachers and their unions, by authors well placed to point to ways to improve the fight back and resistance.'
— Kevin Courtney, Joint General Secretary NEU, Formerly General Secretary NUT

'Unions are not intrinsically powerful. Their strength and effectiveness only come from the extent to which the membership is engaged and active on a permanent basis. This text examines the elements needed to harness this potential: articulate nimble leadership at all levels, robust democratic practices, and strong local workplace structures. The authors have used their experiences as activists to examine the theory and practice of union organising in tangible ways using real-life case studies from the UK. However, because *Lessons in Organising* examines some fundamental truths about union campaigning, its messages are universal, highly relevant to other places and other unions including our own.'
— Maurie Mulheron, Immediate Past President, New South Wales Teachers Federation (2012–20) and Angelo Gavrielatos, Current President New South Wales Teachers Federation (2020–present)

'This book is an important contribution to the development of education unionism. We're reminded of the vital role of workplace organisation, failure of social partnership, and the need for an active rank and file in order to fight neoliberalism in education.'
— Henry Fowler & Robert Poole, Co-founders, Strike Map

'The crisis of organised labour is not reserved to the United States. Through this book we are introduced to the crisis in Britain and the steps that have been taken to renew and transform trade unionism into a twenty-first-century movement! Welcome to an in depth look at the challenges and possibilities for a different approach to trade unionism.'
— Bill Fletcher Jr, co-author of *Solidarity Divided* and author of *"They're Bankrupting Us" – And Twenty Other Myths about Unions*

'In the face of 40 years of neoliberal state policies, teachers forged professional unity and built workplace organisation in their schools through trade union struggles for improved pay, conditions, and to defend children's education. The authors argue today's crisis-ridden capitalism demands new cross-union co-ordinations – a new shop stewards' movement on the scale of the original movement after 1917, or the Liaison Committee for Defence of Trade Unions in the 1960s – to strengthen working-class solidarity and overcome employers' entrenched power. This accessible book is for any worker seeking new ways to organise class struggle.'
— Alex Gordon, President, the National Union of Rail, Maritime and Transport Workers

'A cogent and passionate case for the continued renewal of teacher trade unionism. It is a renewal that is urgently needed not just to defend living standards and working conditions but to salvage and recreate the very purpose, and values, of education itself.'
— Melissa Benn, author of *School Wars and Life Lessons: The Case for a National Education Service*

'A devastating critique of the battle waged by the government over the purpose of education. The authors rightly argue that education is political and in that sense it's a struggle between workers and the employers over what the future looks like. For this reason, teachers and their unions have been locked in a fight, not only over their own terms and conditions, but for school children not to be just fodder for a system of exploitation. The book is both a history lesson in struggle and a practical organising guide for the future. It's about building a form of trade unionism that's industrially militant with a political campaigning focus so that workers are equipped to renew and rebuild their unions for the struggles ahead.'
—Jane Holgate, author of *Arise: Power, Strategy and Union Resurgence*

'Education workers are at the frontline of sustained attacks on a fully funded, publicly owned education service available free to all. These attacks are evident and experienced across all our sectors – schools, further and adult education, and universities. *Lessons in Organising* provides critical insights into how trade unionists can understand and resist these attacks – not only to defend the pay and conditions of education workers, but to also show how they should organise with ambition, around a much more hopeful and optimistic vision of what genuine lifelong education can – and will – mean for everyone.'
—Jo Grady, UCU General Secretary

'An essential read for anyone who wants to understand the importance of collective resistance against the onslaught of neoliberal ideas in education.'
—Venda Premkumar, District Secretary, Redbridge NEU

'Makes clear the reality of organising in a sector that has been systematically privatised by multiple governments and one where the word vocation is used as an excuse to exploit those working within it. This book also shows that even in difficult circumstances it is possible to resist constant attacks from the mainstream media, government cuts and corporate greed. A must read for those in unions seeking to renew and grow.'
—Sarah Woolley, General Secretary, BFAWU

'This book is a fascinating and insightful contribution on the machinations of organising on the ground, straight from those on the frontline; agitating educators, successful in building density during a period of unprecedented anti-union attacks. A must-read for anyone serious about building worker confidence in education and beyond.'
—Shelly Asquith, TUC Health & Safety Officer and Chair of Stop the War

'The continuing work of teachers across the UK to fight for their schools, demand respect and transform their union is rich with lessons for educators, unionists and organisers everywhere. *Lessons in Organising* understands teachers as workers, rightly placing worksite leaders of the union at the centre of the story. By naming the difficult questions we face with a clarity that comes from first hand experience, the authors provide real insights on strategy, union democracy, organisational structure, and the need to hold both radical vision and realistic assessments in our campaigns. This book does not just document the recent history of teachers in England, but provides important direction for all of us committed to strengthening the labour movement and winning the fight against corporate "reform" in education.'
—Matthew Luskin, Director – Organising and Representation Chicago Teachers' Union

Lessons in Organising

What Trade Unionists Can Learn from the War on Teachers

Gawain Little, Ellie Sharp,
Howard Stevenson and David Wilson

PLUTO  PRESS

First published 2023 by Pluto Press
New Wing, Somerset House, Strand, London WC2R 1LA
and Pluto Press Inc.
1930 Village Center Circle, 3-834, Las Vegas, NV 89134

www.plutobooks.com

British Library Cataloguing in Publication Data
A catalogue record for this book is available from the British Library

ISBN 978 0 7453 4522 2   Paperback
ISBN 978 0 7453 4526 0   PDF
ISBN 978 0 7453 4524 6   EPUB

This book is printed on paper suitable for recycling and made from fully
managed and sustained forest sources. Logging, pulping and manufacturing processes are expected to conform to the environmental standards of the
country of origin.

Typeset by Stanford DTP Services, Northampton, England

Simultaneously printed in the United Kingdom and United States of America

Contents

This book is dedicated to Terry Wrigley (1948–2021), an activist and intellectual who always believed that 'another school is possible', William Albin Kyle (1929–2022), a linguist, lover of books and an adored grandfather who proved that learning is lifelong and should be cherished, and William Bryce (1920–2000), a bricklayer by trade, and one of life's natural teachers.

Abbreviations

ALTARF	All London Teachers Against Racism and Fascism
ASOS	Action Short of Strike Action
ATL	Association of Teachers and Lecturers
BBC	British Broadcasting Corporation
BETT	British Educational Training and Technology
BLM	Black Lives Matter
CA	California
CORE	Caucus of Rank and File Educators
CTU	Chicago Teachers' Union
DfE	Department for Education
DOI	Digital Objective Identifier
ed.	editor
edn	edition
eds	editors
EEE	*Educational Excellence Everywhere*
GCSE	General Certificate of Secondary Education
GERM	Global Education Reform Movement
GM	Grant Maintained
GMB	General Municipal Boilermakers' Union
GTVO	Get The Vote Out
HCT	Human Capital Theory
HMSO	Her Majesty's Stationery Office
IAC	Interim Advisory Committee
ILEA	Inner London Education Authority
LGBT+	Lesbian, Gay, Bisexual and Transgender +
MA	Massachusetts
MAT	Multi Academy Trust
MP	Member of Parliament
NASUWT	National Association of School Masters Union of Women Teachers
NES	National Education Service
NEU	National Education Union

NFER	National Foundation for Educational Research
NJ	New Jersey
NUET	National Union of Elementary Teachers
NUT	National Union of Teachers
NY	New York
Ofsted	Office for Standards in Education
PhD	Doctor of Philosophy
SAGE	Scientific Advisory Group for Emergencies
STRB	School Teachers' Review Body
TUC	Trades Union Congress
TV	Television
TVEI	Technical and Vocational Education Initiative
UK	United Kingdom
USA	United States of America
UTLA	United Teachers of Los Angeles

Acknowledgements

This book, like the process it describes, is the product of collective endeavour. The four names that appear on the cover represent one part of that collective. However, the whole process of writing would not have been possible without the many conversations, discussion groups, organising campaigns and industrial actions we participated in with union colleagues too many to name, or without the support of friends and comrades.

We would like to thank by name the following, who read, commented on, discussed or contributed data for parts of the text: Nina Bascia, Mollie Brown, Shana Carquez, Emma Davis, Emily Donnelly, Sophie Evans, Henry Fowler, Bill Fletcher Jr, Angelo Gavrielatos, Aretha Green, Emma Hardy, Lorraine Hunte, Ken Jones, Phil Katz, Alex Kenny, Fay Lockett, Grant MacDonald, Michael MacNeil, Lindsey McDowell, Roger McKenzie, Justine Mercer, Maurie Mulheron, Robert O'Connell, Dan Ross, Alex Snowdon, Darren Turner, Ciaran Walsh and Tracy Walsh. Thanks also to John Dixon. Special thanks go to: Bob Carter, Ben Chacko, Kevin Courtney, Mary Davis, Jane Holgate, John Kelly, Paul McGarr, Dai Morgan and Carly Slingsby. Needless to say, we are entirely responsible for the final contents.

We would also like to express our thanks to all the staff at Pluto Press, but in particular David Castle for his faith in our project as well as his invaluable advice. Finally, and certainly not least of all, we would like to thank Catherine, Rosa and Clara Little, Sarah Farquhar, Susan Munroe, Kate Miller and Alexander and Anais Wilson for their love and support throughout the writing process.

1

Introduction

Gove on 'war footing' with teaching unions expected to launch industrial action.[1]

In mid-2012, one of the authors of this book was contacted out of the blue by a civil servant in the Department for Education (DfE) and invited to the department's offices in Sanctuary Buildings, London to discuss his research on teacher unions. What was expected to be a short informal meeting with a curious junior official turned out to be a lengthy meeting with several senior officials. After a summary of the research, the questions of those present quickly zeroed in on measures of union strength in schools, including membership density, workplace representative density and a battery of related questions.

Although the focus of the officials' interest was clear, the wider purpose of the meeting was not, and nor was it ever fully explained. Perhaps that was one reason why the officials were not provided with the information they were looking for, and why the meeting ended with polite goodbyes, but no subsequent follow-up from either side.

Later in the same year, an annual survey of teacher opinion (the so-called *Teacher Voice Omnibus*[2]), commissioned and paid for by the DfE, was used to find answers to many of the very same questions that had been put to the researcher some months earlier. The published report claimed the purpose of the survey was to identify 'whether the current work to rule by teachers [in relation to workload] was having an impact in respondents' schools, but it was not clear why a large, expensive survey was being used to collect information about a dispute that could have been collected more quickly, easily and cheaply simply by emailing headteachers.

That confusion was cleared up on 9 December 2012 when a number of newspapers closely aligned to the Conservative Party led with front-page headlines claiming the Department for Education had been placed on a 'war footing' by Secretary of State Michael Gove in anticipation of a dispute with teacher unions. The headline in the *Daily Mail* from that day opens this chapter, while the *Sunday Times* on the same day led with 'Gove's war over pay for teachers'.[3]

In December 2012, teachers' unions had not even seen the proposals that were to be presented by the 'independent' review body that makes recommendations on teachers' pay (in the absence of a proper system of collective bargaining), let alone had a chance to respond to any proposals. But at that time, the government's education department had already been mobilised and was briefing sympathetic newspapers that it was on a 'war footing'. Indeed, as this brief outline of events makes clear, senior officials in the Department for Education had clearly been preparing their battle plans for several months, dating at least as far back as the meeting with the researcher, possibly longer.

This is what we mean by the 'war on teachers'. If the language seems hyperbolic, we make no apology. The language we have adopted is no more than the very same language used by the government to describe its relations with the democratic organisations that represent the vast majority of the education workforce.[4] It is *their* language, and it is a language with a long history. As far back as the 1960s, the right-wing authors of a series of policy papers were describing their campaign against progressive primary education and comprehensive schooling as a 'fight for education' (Cox and Dyson, 1969). It is a war that has lasted decades, and which they continue to wage relentlessly, whether in the form of attacks on working conditions or ever more strenuous efforts to take control of what teachers teach, and how they teach it. In many senses, it is a war that has assumed a global form (Compton and Weiner, 2008).

The earliest skirmishes in this extended confrontation began when the political right mobilised to push back against the expansion of the post-war welfare state. In education, these developments had been significant. The Plowden Report published in 1967[5] presaged radical developments in child-centred primary school pedagogy, while secondary education was increasingly being modelled on comprehensive lines (rejecting the selective system of grammar and secondary modern schools). In the years that followed, there was a growth of anti-racist and anti-sexist education initiatives within several local authorities, in particular in the Inner London Education Authority. We are clear that these initial developments were often tentative and uneven, and we are not suggesting this was a 'golden age' for progressive education. However, it was a period when the direction of travel pointed to the very real possibilities of an education system built on principles of social justice and democracy.

It was precisely these possibilities that were identified as so dangerous by those at the time referred to as the 'New Right'. Education needed to be restored to its original purpose, ensuring that students had the right skills and dispositions to fill their designated slots in the labour market. There was a real concern about what was seen as the 'over-education' of working-class students in a social system that could not match their aspirations. One senior civil servant summarised the argument:

> We are in a period of considerable social change. There may be social unrest, but we can cope with the Toxteth's. But if we have a highly educated and idle population we may possibly anticipate more serious social conflict. *People must be educated once more to know their place.*
> (quoted in Simon, 1984, p. 21; emphasis added)

This meant that the education system needed to manage working-class aspirations while also inculcating appropriate notions of 'individual responsibility', 'Englishness' and respect for what are today referred to as 'fundamental British values'. Crucially, it needed to reproduce divisions based on sex and race, and the ideologies which sustain them, including patriarchy, 'family values' and a racist reading of history that extolled the virtues of empire. Working-class kids needed to be trained for working-class jobs and a working-class experience of precarious contracts and periodic joblessness.

This is why education is political. It is always political, because it is fundamentally a struggle over what the future can look like, and it is for this reason that the ruling class has waged a relentless battle against the ideas that began to emerge in the post-war period, and which are seen as such a threat to the stability of the prevailing social system. It is inevitable, therefore, that teachers have found themselves in the front line of these struggles, as it is in the daily actions of teachers that competing visions of education emerge. The battle over the purposes of education plays out principally as a struggle over the curriculum (what is taught), but emerges practically as a struggle for the control of teachers' work, as it is through the pedagogical practices of teachers that the curriculum is enacted and curriculum aims are realised.

After simmering for many years, the 'war on teachers' erupted into the open in the mid-1980s when the teacher unions were engaged in a protracted dispute with local authority employers and central government over pay and working conditions. Ever since that time, the nature of the conflict has ebbed and flowed, sometimes breaking out into the open (such as in 2012/2013), but often assuming a less conspicuous form. In this book, we use the ideas of Antonio Gramsci to distinguish between a 'war of movement' and a 'war of position'. Gramsci was an early leader of the Italian Communist Party who was imprisoned by Mussolini's fascist government in 1926. He was a political leader and organiser, but is most famous for his *Prison Notebooks* (1971), in which he reflected on revolutionary strategy in the context of an increasingly complex capitalist society. Gramsci was technically released from imprisonment in 1937, but by this time he was so ill he could not leave the clinic in which he was incarcerated. He died a few days after his 'release' – murdered by fascism (for a full discussion of Gramsci's political and educational ideas, see Stevenson, 2023).

Gramsci's notion of a war of movement was a very direct confrontation between opposing forces, often lasting for a limited amount of time. In contrast, a war of position reflected a less visible, but constant and ongoing, struggle over the ideas that dominate our lives and frame how people make sense of 'reality'. Gramsci was clear that it is important to understand both types of conflict, and that both can co-exist. However, in complex capitalist societies, where everyday ideas about what is considered as 'the way things are' are deeply embedded, the importance of ideological struggle against what Gramsci called the accepted 'common sense' must never be underestimated. What may be resisted initially can easily become normalised, and what may be accepted reluctantly can, over time become acceptable – unless those ideas are contested and challenged.

We present this war on teachers as both a war of movement, erupting at particular moments, and a relentless and ongoing war of position in which the political right has sought to establish a new 'common sense' in education based on competition, privatisation and cultural conservativism. Central to this new common sense are the efforts to demonise trade union organisation and collective action.

Given the scale of the resources the political right has been able to mobilise, it cannot come as a surprise that its efforts have secured significant results. The state, the media, and often sections of the Labour Party, have been available to reinforce the neoliberal agenda in education. Consequently, the system has been reorganised in a way that largely eliminates local democratic control of schools and creates a market in which students and teachers are forced to compete against each other in a race that nobody can win. Meanwhile, teachers and other education workers see their workloads rise inexorably, their pay reduced in real terms, and their professional judgement curtailed by micro-management and the crude application of metrics used to make judgements about performance. Both student and teacher have become units to measure in a system that has been progressively dehumanised.

But this is not a war that has been won – far from it. Every day, there are teachers and support staff working in schools who refuse to accept the dehumanisation of the system and who find small but important ways to challenge the logic of the exam factories[6] in which they work. Many work hard to put students first, fighting hardest for those who face the greatest challenges and oppressions. These individual acts of resistance are everywhere, and they sustain hope in a system that can seem hopeless.

But the war has also not been won because despite all the efforts of the state to defeat and destroy teachers' collective organisations, education trade unions remain formidable, with high levels of membership across the sector and considerable organisational capacity. Teachers and other education workers continue to join trade unions, and education unions continue to assert considerable power and influence. Nowhere was this illustrated more clearly than during the COVID-19 pandemic, when unions in schools forced a chaotic and incompetent government into a number of humiliating U-turns, but most conspicuously in January 2021.

In December 2020, the UK was in the grip of a second wave of the Coronavirus pandemic. However, despite raging transmission rates, and linked mortality figures, the Secretary of State for Education insisted that all primary schools (except those in London) should open for in-person teaching on 4 January 2021. Education workers in primary schools faced the rapidly approaching new term with a mixture of anxiety and incredulity. They knew from their previous experience how inadequate the social distancing arrangements in their schools were, and in the light of transmission rates at the time, the actions of government seemed reckless. But what to do?

The terrain shifted dramatically on Saturday 2 January, 48 hours before the start of the new term. The National Education Union (NEU) contacted its members and workplace representatives, having issued a press release stating:

> Today the National Education Union has taken the difficult decision to advise its members in primary and special needs schools, and early years settings, that it is unsafe to return to work on Monday.[7]

The union urged its members to invoke Section 44 of the Health and Safety at Work Act to argue that their workplace was not safe, so they would only be willing to work remotely. Workplace representatives were provided with instructions about how to organise members collectively around what was an individual legal right and communicate this position to their headteachers.

The following day, Sunday 3 January, Prime Minister Boris Johnson appeared on the high-profile *Marr Show* (a weekly politics TV programme) and indicated he had 'no doubt' schools were safe and that parents should 'absolutely' send their children into school the next day.[8] However, by Monday evening (4 January), as the impact of the NEU's action had become apparent, Boris Johnson made an 8 p.m. televised address to the nation in which he accepted that schools were 'vectors of transmission' and announced they would move immediately online until at least the middle of February. This was unquestionably the most dramatic climbdown by the government during the whole of the pandemic, when even its 80-seat parliamentary majority could not insulate it from the political fallout that forced its retreat. It was a moment when the interests of people – children, workers and communities – were put before the economic interests of big business.

This extraordinary series of events marked the moment when the National Education Union (formed in 2017 out of an amalgamation of the National Union of Teachers [NUT] and the Association of Teachers and Lecturers [ATL]) was able to mobilise its members to force a powerful government into a humiliating retreat. The union's ability to organise through the pandemic generated enormous levels of member engagement and support. The NEU was by no means unique as a trade union in attracting increased membership during the pandemic as workers across the economy sought protection from employers who placed profits and organisational goals before the safety of their employees. However, by any measure, the NEU's engagement with its members was extraordinary. At the height of the pandemic, the union had recruited 50,000 new members and 4,500 new workplace representatives. Online organising utilised new digital communications, and in a single meeting organised using Zoom the union had an audience of 400,000 members and supporters. This was the organisational strength that delivered the victory on the 4 January 2021 and many of the other less conspicuous, but highly significant, achievements in the campaign to keep schools safe for students, staff and their communities.

In this book, we seek to describe, understand and explain the context and background that led up to the events discussed above, as one battle in the wider war on teachers, but a battle that was won by educators. It is important to recognise that the achievements the union secured, and the levels of collective action that these were built on, did not appear as a set of purely spontaneous developments. The Coronavirus pandemic shifted the terrain for union organising, but this is not enough to explain what happened in January 2021. Rather, it is important to understand the strategic choices adopted by the NUT,[9] and then the NEU, during a period of more than ten years, to understand why the union was able to organise so effectively during the period of the pandemic. This is key to learning the lessons of the war on teachers.

In presenting our analysis, we draw on a framework first developed by Bob Carter, Howard Stevenson and Rowena Passy (2010) in their study of teacher unions in the period of the social partnership in England and Wales (2003–2010). At the time, Carter and colleagues identified one of the strategic options available to trade unions as *rapprochement*, whereby unions work with the grain of the prevailing system, seeking to secure the best deal for workers, but without fundamentally challenging the system itself. This was arguably the dominant thinking in the NUT for much of its post-war history. It delivered some significant gains in a period of social democratic consensus and welfare state expansion, but delivered little when that consensus collapsed and the war on teachers broke out in earnest. This was when the state became openly antagonistic to teacher union organisation. In contrast, the same study identified *resistance* as an approach that sought to challenge the system more profoundly, often by confronting it with industrial action. However, in a hostile environment for trade unions, with system fragmentation and legal obstacles, it appeared increasingly difficult to mobilise the type and scale of action necessary to secure significant gains. As the war on teachers intensified, a strategy of resistance had obvious immediate attractions, but it was also inadequate to the task. Resistance alone, without wider change in trade unions themselves, was not enough.

Rather, Carter and colleagues made the case for union *renewal* as a (necessary) strategic choice for trade unions. Renewal absolutely recognised the need for resistance, but argued that this must be based around active union-building that connected with union members in their workplaces. By emphasising the importance of workplace issues – members' control of the workplace labour process – the union assumes everyday relevance rather than appearing remote and fashioned only for individual grievances and intermittent set-piece battles. Resistance involved unions trying to deliver more action (often when the scale of the action was diminishing), whereas union renewal required a change in the union itself in order to strengthen the capacity of the union to deliver more effective action. The nature of the war on teachers, both its locus and focus, required a transformation of the union in order to be able to build the resistance required to challenge the neoliberal restructuring of schools. This is what we mean here by 'renewal'.

We offer an analysis of the NUT and NEU's experience of renewal, and indeed the unions' version of renewal, which builds on the starting point offered by the Carter study. Here we elaborate on the experience of the NEU/NUT as a means of developing a more fully formed conception of what union renewal must mean. We believe there is much to be learned from the experience of the NEU/NUT, positive and otherwise, that has a relevance far beyond the education sector and the work of education activists. The challenges that have confronted the education unions are by no means unique – indeed, many industrial sectors have faced more significant problems as part of a war on the organised working class. Nobody reading this book will be unaware of, or unaffected by, the crisis that continues to confront organised labour and the trade union movement. At the same time, the NEU/NUT's experience of renewal is not unique either. In the UK, trade union membership decline is beginning to reverse, and this is a trend that pre-dated Coronavirus and any lockdown-related surge in membership identified above. What is more, the rebuilding of union organisation extends far beyond the usual metrics of membership growth, but increasingly reflects new forms of trade unionism that are based on vibrant grassroots organisation and workplace organising. With the potential of the economy moving into a period of high inflation and a consequent increase in union mobilisation and industrial action, some of these developments may become even more significant. There may be signs of a new unionism – but whatever the circumstances, it remains embryonic and uncertain, and hence we believe it is vital that trade union activists seeking to give life to these developments in their own contexts take every opportunity to learn from each other. The crisis that continues to face organised labour, and the ongoing war against workers, require us all to engage in open discussion about our experiences and to try to understand what can work, and in what circumstances.

The need for union renewal in some form, no matter how it is labelled, is now widely accepted as the crisis of labour has deepened. However, there is an obvious danger that the language of renewal is no more than warm words in which the language of action is used to camouflage caution and inaction, or to legitimize actions so bland as to be meaningless. We hope this book can help develop collective thinking and learning in the labour movement and share experiences and analyses that can deepen our understanding of what sort of union renewal is required to build union power and confront the challenges facing organised labour.

TEACHERS AS WORKERS AND TEACHING AS WORK: THE SIGNIFICANCE OF CLASS, SEX AND RACE

In this book, the language we have adopted largely refers to teaching, teachers and teacher trade unionism. This was not a straightforward decision, because our political commitment is to a form of trade union organising that seeks to organise on an industrial basis, uniting all the workers in a workplace, regardless of their specific role. However, where we refer to teachers, rather than using what can be considered as the more inclusive terms of educator, education worker or similar, it is an intentional choice. This is because 'teaching' and 'teachers' capture most accurately what the political right has been determined to attack. It is the *act of teaching* that the right sees as so dangerous. There has been a war on teachers precisely because it is the *act of teaching* that is so potentially subversive and which therefore must be constantly monitored and controlled. Using this formulation in this way does not restrict our interest to those narrowly defined as 'qualified teachers', but rather recognises the contribution of all workers who teach and support teaching.

This approach to teaching and teachers is rooted in our analysis of teachers' work as a labour process in which teachers as workers are engaged in a struggle with employers for control of the work itself – the form and content of the work, how the work is evaluated and rewarded, and who gets to decide these issues. In popular imagery, teaching is often presented as a 'vocation', and teachers are members of a profession. These are important issues, but they are frequently invoked by managers to exhort staff to 'go the extra mile' or to condemn collective action because it is 'unprofessional'. These notions deliberately obscure the real nature of work by removing the boundaries between what counts as work and what does not. In this context, the teacher can never work hard enough, and efforts to draw any boundary around work time can be represented as 'not caring', or not being 'professional'.

Our starting point is much more straightforward, and draws on Raewyn Connell's simple assertion:

> Teachers are workers, teaching is work, and the school is a workplace. These simple facts are often forgotten.
>
> (Connell, 1985, p. 69)

Under capitalism, the nature of the employment relationship is fundamentally exploitative, with employers seeking to maximise their share of the value workers create. Teachers' work performs a crucial role in equipping workers with the skills required by employers for capital accumulation, while teachers also perform a key ideological function by promoting in workers appropriate values, attitudes and dispositions. Of course, these roles are always contested and challenged, and teachers do not simply act as functionaries. That is why teachers' work is always a site of struggle. However, in these two important respects teachers' work is critical to the functioning of capital, so the state will always seek to assert control over the work that teachers do – not only trying to drive up 'output' (increasingly measured by standardised test scores), but also trying to control the content of what teachers can teach. Moreover, as a large, labour-intensive industrial sector (financed in part by taxes on profits), efforts to drive output up will simultaneously be accompanied by efforts to drive costs down (processes that have intensified as globalised capitalist competition has accelerated). In this sense, teachers face the same struggle as workers elsewhere in the economy – workers work for employers who seek to maximise 'productivity', or put more simply, try to get 'more for less'. The more that schools resemble private businesses competing in a market, the more sharply these pressures are experienced by teachers and all staff in schools. Hence the need to understand teachers' labour process as the site of what Goodrich (1920/1975) called the 'frontier of control' between employers' and workers' struggle for control of work. But fundamentally, and returning to Connell's assertion above, teachers are workers, engaged in a labour process that seeks to exploit their labour, within a system which subjugates their labour to the broader needs of a particular social system. Challenging this situation ultimately requires teachers to recognise their collective interests as members of the working class, to act collectively with other members of the class, and to fundamentally confront efforts to shape education in ways that are detrimental to young people and the wider interests of the working class.

Within this system of exploitation, not all workers are treated equally. Some face super-exploitation – experiencing a higher rate of exploitation due to lower wages, unpaid labour and/or being forced into insecure and lower-paid jobs – on the basis of sexist and racist oppression. This oppression is sustained by the ideologies of sexism and racism, which have a material impact on conditions of labour for women and Black workers (Davis, 2020). If we look at the historical development of capitalism, we see the labour of enslaved people, the super-exploitation of migrant and colonial populations, and the unpaid labour of women in the home written into every step. As shown by the Trades Union Congress (TUC) UK survey into the experiences of Black workers[10] and the persistence of the gender pay gap,[11] racism and sexism continue to have a huge impact at an economic level. The super-exploitation of Black and women workers has been a fundamental condition of capitalist exploitation since its very beginning, and the oppressive ideologies of racism and sexism which sustain this situation are fundamentally entwined within the capitalist system (Bhattacharyya, 2018; D'Atri, 2022).

In education, this oppression can be seen in the job segregation and gender pay gap faced by women teachers (a gap that increases with age and seniority so that male senior leaders are paid over 11% more than their female equivalents[12]). It is also clearly evident in the barriers experienced by Black teachers in their quest for career progression.[13] Furthermore, it is important to acknowledge that such barriers exist within the trade union movement, and that many members experience structural obstacles to their full and equal participation in the organisation.

The consequences of the racist and sexist division of labour in schools is to condemn women and Black workers disproportionately to the lowest-paid, most insecure work. However, it can also be seen on the other side of the teaching relationship as these oppressive ideologies are reinforced and recreated through the school system. In 2017, a joint report by the NEU and UK Feminista[14] found that over a third of female students at mixed-sex schools had personally experienced some form of sexual harassment. At the same time, 64% of teachers in mixed-sex secondary schools hear sexist language in school on at least a weekly basis. A quarter of all secondary school teachers say they witness gender stereotyping and discrimination in their school on a daily basis. Similarly, the role of schools in the transmission and crystallisation of racial inequality in education has long been acknowledged (Richardson, 2005), and more recently, the racist nature of school exclusions has become widely recognised.[15]

This is not to say that these ideas are not contested. Initiatives such as the NEU Anti-Racism Charter[16] and the Breaking the Mould project[17] represent just some of the educator-led initiatives to challenge racism and sexism, but these are systemic ideologies and practices of oppression. They therefore require systemic solutions. It is also important to recognise that sexism and racism cannot simply be reduced to questions of class. As Mary Davis (2020) argues:

> these are not simply mechanisms for keeping Black and women workers in a subordinate position since, as oppressive ideologies, they cut across class boundaries and depend, as all ideologies do, on their universalism. Hence, they impinge on the lives of all Black people and women, regardless of class, and determine society's perception of race and gender.
>
> (p. vi)

These questions of class, sex and race underpin our analysis.

TEACHER TRADE UNIONISM:
INTRODUCING THE NATIONAL EDUCATION UNION

This book provides a case study of a single trade union – the National Education Union – and one of its predecessor unions – the NUT. The National Education Union was formed in 2017 as an amalgamation of the Association of Teachers and Lecturers and the National Union of Teachers. The NEU is organised into geographical districts and employer-facing branches (known respectively as associations and divisions in the NUT), which are in many cases coterminous.[18] Policy is decided by an annual delegate conference and the union's national executive is responsible for the implementation of policy in between conferences. On formation, the NEU had 450,000 members, and it is the largest education union in Europe. The union is a member of the Trades Union Congress.

The structure of school-sector trade unionism in the UK is notoriously complex, not least because education policy is devolved to individual nations within the UK. Education policy can look quite different across the individual nations of England, Scotland, Wales and Northern Ireland.[19] Different unions have formed to represent different geographical areas, while different unions also organise in different sectors (for example, schools, post-16 colleges, further education colleges) as well as different types of employees (classroom teachers, support staff, school leaders). For the most part, many of these differences may be considered at the margins. What is more striking about school-sector industrial relations is that for most employees in the school sector in all the nations of the UK, there are multiple unions seeking to represent the same groups of workers and competing for the same members. This is a form of multi-unionism known as 'competitive' unionism (because several unions are literally competing to recruit the same potential members). It contrasts with many other countries where multi-unionism in the education sector is a form of 'adjacent' unionism (for example, in New Zealand two different unions represent primary and secondary school teachers respectively, whereas in Australia the distinction is between separate unions recruiting in public and independent – that is, private – schools). Recognising the specific nature of multi-unionism in the school sector in England is important in understanding the terrain on which the activities of education unions take place. In recent years, one of the most significant developments in trade union membership in the English school sector has been the growth of unions who recruit only school leaders (two unions only represent school leaders, whereas others recruit across the teaching profession). This trend has almost certainly been driven by an education system that has opened up a divide within the teaching profession between managers (now commonly referred to as 'leaders') and those who are classroom-based. Another key development has been the increase in union membership among support staff, a development not unconnected to their rapid expansion in numbers after 'workforce remodelling' in the period 2003–2010, and the intensification of their work and continued low pay subsequently. Most support staff have been represented by one of the big general unions (the public service union, Unison), but for many years the ATL also recruited support staff. It followed that when the NUT and ATL amalgamated, one of the consequences was to make the new union a *de facto* industrial union (organising all those who work in the relevant sector). Growth in union membership among support staff has been one of the most dramatic developments in the recent period.

Competitive multi-unionism has led to significant organisational division among teachers in the UK, and this in turn has contributed to tactical and strategic divisions. This has meant that, in spite of high union density in the sector, teacher unions have been much weaker, industrially and politically, than they would otherwise be. The amalgamation of the ATL and NUT to form the National Education Union in 2017 was a significant and positive development in building unity across the education workforce, thereby strengthening the position of education workers. This, combined with the fact that the new union inherited the ATL's industrial union tradition of organising all education workers regardless of role, makes it a hugely significant step forward for the trade union movement in education. In different ways, several of us have played a role in making the amalgamation between the two unions happen. However, this book is not the place to explore that process in any detail, because to do the story justice would require a book in itself!

In this book, we trace developments that pre-date the formation of the NEU but were a feature of one of its predecessor organisations, the NUT. The NEU is clearly a new and distinctive union, already developing its own culture and history. However, the new union is also a product of both of its predecessor organisations, and here we argue that important elements of the NUT's renewal agenda have been further developed in the new organisation. It would be equally possible to write a book tracing the continuities from the ATL to the NEU, but that is not the purpose of this book, and we would not be best placed to write it. Our histories and experiences are rooted in the NUT.

What became the NUT was formed as the National Union of Elementary Teachers (NUET) in 1870, in the same year when the state legislated to establish a system of public education. The union was geographically situated in England and Wales. The NUET was focused on recruiting and representing teachers, and campaigned for an appropriately qualified profession. However, divisions within the school system were in turn reflected within the profession, and from the outset unionism within the sector was characterised by fragmentation, splits and breakaways. These differences often reflected the gendered nature of the teaching profession and the job segregation faced by women within teaching. For example, one major competitor union was formed in 1922 when it split from the NUT in opposition to its newly adopted policy in favour of equal pay for women.

In 1889, the NUET became the National Union of Teachers, reflecting the growth of secondary schooling. The union was the largest in the sector, but over time this numerical dominance diminished.

The NUT's first strike action took place in 1896 in Portsmouth, when the union supported members taking action against a much-despised system of payment by results. However, the NUT's first national strike did not take place until 1969, when economic crisis, and its associated inflation, began to hit pay and pensions. This was the period when the NUT began to take on the familiar form of an industrial trade union, rather than acting as a professional association that also bargained over pay and working conditions. The NUT joined the TUC in 1970, and throughout the 1970s and 1980s there was a growth of grassroots organisation. One manifestation of this was the emergence of several left groups (or 'caucuses'), and this type of grassroots left activity has been a significant feature of both the NUT and the NEU since that time. For much of the time this was framed around a division between members of the Socialist Teachers' Alliance and a 'Broad Left', although in the 1990s a third group emerged, the Campaign for a Democratic and Fighting Union, and this acted as an alternative pole for activist support. All of these groups continue to function within the new union, alongside others that have formed and re-formed over time. At the current time, it is not possible to discern what form this type of activity will assume in the new union, although it is already clear that new groups are forming and coalescing, most obviously the NEU Left, but also other groups such as the Education Solidarity Network. It is not our intention here to provide a detailed analysis of all the groups that exist, or have existed, in the different unions. It is, however, important to understand that this type of self-organising within the NUT, and now the NEU, is an important feature of the union's organising culture. Left caucuses have historically been an important current of activism and a valuable source of critical thinking within the union, and this tradition remains relevant to understanding the new union.

FOCUS AND STRUCTURE OF THE BOOK

In this book, we seek to analyse critically the 'turn to organising' in the trade union movement by drawing on the specific experiences of the NEU and NUT to help understand this experience in terms of lessons to be learned and conclusions to be drawn. We show how the commitment to organising has been absolutely central to the renewal of the NEU/NUT, but that the experience also reveals the limitations of such an approach, and that organising, narrowly defined, may be considered necessary but not sufficient for developing a trade unionism that can effectively challenge neoliberal hegemony. There is therefore a need to go 'beyond organising'.

In Chapter 2, we briefly discuss the crisis of organised labour and identify the trade union responses that have developed as a consequence. In particular, we describe the failed efforts to promote social partnership and take comfort from the 'turn to organising' that we have seen across the wider trade union movement. However, we raise concerns that approaches to organising are often too bland, or too formulaic, to be of genuine value to trade union activists seeking to build union power in the workplace. The chapter concludes by setting out how the NUT sought to connect theory and practice as it engaged with ideas and research to help shape its own organising strategy in the specific context of the English school system

In Chapter 3, we provide a historical overview of the war on teachers in England. We hope this will be of value to readers who work in other employment sectors or who are not familiar with the English system of public education. The chapter will also be of interest to those working in the English education system but who may not be familiar with the analysis presented. A feature of the current school system is that critical analysis from within is not encouraged, including within teacher education programmes, and it is no accident that the analysis we present here is not widely discussed as part of teacher education courses. The chapter provides essential context for the discussion of the NEU/NUT that follows.

In Chapters 4, 5 and 6 we deal in detail with the experiences of the NEU/NUT. Chapter 4 discusses the union's focus on workplace organising, and in Chapter 5 we show how the union built on its organising base, and has gone 'beyond organising' to become a more outward-facing campaigning union that has sought to challenge directly the dominance of neoliberal hegemony in English state education.[20] In Chapter 6, we discuss the NEU's experience of the pandemic and show how the union was able to bring together the approaches we set out in Chapters 4 and 5 to mobilise on an unprecedented scale. We also discuss the need to further develop these strategies and the steps required to continue to build the collective power of union members, in particular by focusing on the need to develop leadership at every level of trade union organisation.

In the final chapter, we return the debate to the broader trade union movement and connect the experience of the NEU/NUT to that of the wider movement. We discuss the sort of actions that will be necessary to build a genuine new unionism across the labour movement. We set out our 'lessons in organising' – not as a formula or set of instructions, but in the spirit of critical education, as a set of experiences which can generate collective discussion and from which collective learning can follow.

We hope the different experiences and perspectives we bring as two NEU activists, a researcher and a union official help offer a rounded view of the developments we discuss and provide a balanced assessment of the issues. We are keen to acknowledge weaknesses, errors and limitations, and the fact that despite some of the very real successes we discuss, serious problems continue to face education workers which can only be addressed by building a stronger union able to take effective action, locally and nationally. We are not complacent about the need for that action to take place on a more substantial scale, and we hope that this book can make a contribution to the development of such a collective response. The book is not written as a manual for activists, but we hope it will be an inspiration to action. There is a world to win, but changing it requires understanding it, and we hope this book can contribute to that understanding.

2

The Crisis of Organised Labour

The labour movement in the UK is in crisis. The crisis is deep, and is the product of many years of decline. The reality is that on all key indicators (union membership, density, bargaining coverage and industrial action), the data point to declining union power, influence and impact. In the UK, total union membership declined by 50% between 1980 and 2016, although in the years since then the trend has shown signs of reversing,[1] and changing economic conditions have certainly contributed to an upturn in strike action.[2] When data for industrial disputes were released in 2018,[3] they detailed the sixth lowest number of strike days since records began (1891), the second lowest numbers of workers involved since records began (1893) and the second lowest number of stoppages since records began (1930). What industrial action took place was overwhelmingly dominated by the education sector (66% of all strike action), of which the universities pensions dispute was a large part. On almost all these indicators, the gap between public sector and private sector experience is considerable. The danger is that aggregate data can mask a profound crisis in private sector trade unionism, while Bob Carter and Roger Kline (2017) have argued that there is no cause for complacency among public sector trade unionists either. The problems are everywhere. Circumstances may change, and trends can reverse, but whatever the context, it is clear that the task of rebuilding union power is a substantial one that will require labour movement activists to make important strategic choices.

This chapter provides an analysis of the 'crisis of labour', and the ways in which rising union power in the post-war years was first halted, and then reversed, by a ruling class intent on reasserting 'management's right to manage', whether in private industry or in the state sector. This is because the crisis of labour we describe, which assumes many forms in different contexts, is not an accidental development, or the consequence of social and technological developments that are often presented as the inevitable forward march of 'progress'. Rather, the crisis faced by organised labour derives directly from the efforts by the capitalist class to weaken labour's ability to resist its own exploitation and, in turn, to strengthen capital's ability to generate and extract profit.

The chapter outlines the dominant responses of the trade union movement as it has wrestled with retreat and sought to resume labour's forward march. For heuristic purposes, this is presented as a choice between 'social partnership' and 'institutional organising', although, as we argue here, the reality suggests a more complex relationship between the two than a simple either/or binary. The chapter concludes by identifying and discussing a range of theories, ideas and research linked to debates about organising and union renewal that have played a particular role in shaping the NUT and NEU's response to the crisis in state education – a crisis that has had profound implications for education workers and education trade unions.

UNDERSTANDING THE CRISIS

In the post-war years, capital, organised labour and the state established a new settlement underpinned by a welfare state, full employment and collective bargaining. According to this compromise, trade unions were crucial to securing an element of 'fairness' for workers in the workplace, but they were not intended to challenge the system that was the source of the injustice. Inequality and exploitation, as the basis of the employment relationship, were to be mitigated, but not eliminated. However, in the context of a relatively long period of economic expansion, and a correspondingly tight labour market, workplace organising by grassroots trade unionists flourished and was able to make significant organisational advances as well as win material gains from employers. Strong workplace-based trade union organisation (mostly in engineering and manufacturing) gave organised workers considerable leverage and allowed a strong shop stewards movement to challenge managerial authority and to push back what Carter Goodrich (1920/1975) had called the 'frontier of control' in favour of shop floor workers.[4] At this time, shop stewards were closely accountable to their immediate workmates and union members, but they generally enjoyed considerable autonomy from their official union. Hence, the high levels of 'unofficial' industrial action.[5] At the time, Allan Flanders (1970, p. 51), a highly influential industrial relations academic, referred to the situation as 'anarchy in the workplace', with this image popularised in the media and by politicians. It was against this background, alongside the slow-down of the long boom of capitalist expansion, that the employers and state began to counter-mobilise.

At this time, the concern was largely focused on industrial relations in private sector industry, as this was where the 'problem' of a powerful and largely autonomous shop steward's movement was perceived to be. The response of the state was to seek to undermine the power of shop stewards by establishing a more formalised system of industrial relations with a stronger emphasis on conducting industrial relations through agreed procedures. Where possible, such agreements should be centralised (to reduce the scope for local negotiation) and trade union representatives were to be supported in these more formal processes by having access to paid release for union duties and time off to undertake union training ('facilities time'[6]). Trade unions were expected to not only 'play by the rules', but to take remedial action if ever their own members threatened to 'step out of line'.

The development of trade union organisation in the post-war years and the strengthening of collective bargaining arrangements represented a significant advance for the working class. Full employment and real-terms wage growth pointed to a significant and substantial shift in the balance of forces in favour of organised labour. However, the period also highlighted the limitations of an approach to trade union organisation that ultimately favoured accommodation and compromise, and failed to recognise the oppression of women and Black workers and the roots of that oppression in super-exploitation. Indeed, as independent and rank-and-file militancy developed as a serious challenge to the domination of capital, so too did the state mobilise to increasingly intervene in the industrial relations system. This first became apparent during a period of Labour government when a controversial white paper, *In Place of Strife*,[7] proposed radical powers for the state to step in to prevent unofficial industrial action. The proposals were defeated by large-scale trade union resistance, but a Conservative Party election victory in 1970 ensured it was soon followed by legislation seeking to curb union power.

The Industrial Relations Act 1971 ushered in several years of intense class struggle, driven forward by growing networks of grassroots activists within and between industries.[8] In 1974, the Tory Prime Minister, Edward Heath, called a general election in which he explicitly posed the question: *Who governs the country* – striking miners or his administration? In the subsequent election, the Conservatives lost power and the incoming Labour government repealed the 1971 Act. However, this was replaced with Labour's own industrial relations legislation, and by now the experience of the state using legislation to regulate the activities of trade unions was becoming well established.[9] However, state–trade union relations were to become even more blurred when the Labour government at the time, together with the TUC, formally agreed a 'Social Contract' in response to a deepening economic crisis and escalating inflation. This agreement had the dual impact of imposing wage restraint across industries, which drew in the large public-sector bargaining units, but also restraining grassroots activists who sought to challenge their falling real-terms pay. The catastrophic impact on workers' living standards resulted in the 'winter of discontent' in 1978–1979, when 22 million strike days were taken. One important feature of this period was the growing profile of public-sector trade unions in the disputes, many with a majority of women members. Historically highly centralised collective bargaining in the state sector, combined with public sector growth, had resulted in relatively stable industrial relations in sectors such as health, education and local government. In the 1970s, this began to change as public expenditure cuts presaged a new militancy among unions in the sector. However, while demonstrating a high level of combativity, during the 1978/1979 period in particular, it is also the case that an element of demoralisation and political disorientation had begun to seep into grassroots worker organisation across the movement. High-level trade union support for wage restraint divided the trade union movement, while striking against a Labour government, and often Labour local authorities, added to the sense of confusion.

Following the election of Margaret Thatcher as Prime Minister in 1979, the state was engaged in a much more open form of class conflict and the Tories' war on organised workers was clear for all to see. Explicitly anti-trade union legislation was only part of the armoury, with unemployment, privatisation and militarised forms of policing (witness the miners' strike and the News International dispute at Wapping in London) also forming part of the arsenal focused on efforts to crush the power of organised labour. This was a moment when the ruling class went on the offensive against organised workers in an effort to halt, and reverse, the post-war advances secured by the labour movement. It marked the beginning of a period in which every effort was made to create a hostile environment for effective trade union organisation. From this time, trade union rights have continually been eroded through legislation (most recently by the draconian Trade Union Act 2016[10]), while labour's collective bargaining base has been attacked on many fronts (from austerity through to gig working and the emergence of hyper-flexible labour markets). Workplace cultures positively encourage the individualised employee (reinforced through performance-related payment systems), and elaborate exercises in employee 'voice' are used to undermine the independent and democratic voice of organised workers. Should all else fail, bullying managerialism can be relied on to ensure management's authority is maintained.

Before presenting trade union responses to the developments described above, it is important to set out a number of points that underpin our analysis of both the historic crisis of organised labour and the steps necessary to rebuild union power.

The first is the need to recognise the scale of the crisis facing the labour movement. Different issues will play out very differently in different contexts, but there is nothing to be gained by seeking to 'wish away' those factors that make the tasks of union organisers and activists more difficult. The starting point for developing effective strategy is to analyse the world as it actually is and to identify what factors and contextual specificities shape the organising environment, and in what ways. There is no simple relationship between prevailing conditions and the propensity of workers to push back. Clearly, material conditions frame the terrain on which struggles take place, but believing that worker resistance is the inevitable reaction to deteriorating economic conditions not only defies the evidence, but also encourages a deterministic passivity in the movement. Waiting for some undefined 'moment', beyond anyone's control, that at some point will bring forth the required worker response is a dangerous miscalculation.

Second, it is important to recognise that reversing the fortunes of the labour movement cannot solely depend on the election of left leaders to senior positions within unions. This is not to say that left leaderships of unions are unimportant – far from it – but in and of itself, it is not enough to reverse the tide of the decline in union power. In the UK, over a number of years several unions, of very different sizes and sectors, can be described as having 'left' general secretaries, sometimes with a corresponding left presence at the level of national executive bodies. The NEU/ NUT is one such union. Having a 'left leadership' has contributed to many of the positive developments discussed in this book. However, what is clear is that such developments on their own have not been sufficient to bring about the reversal of fortunes required by the labour movement. What has often been missing in unions with elected left leaders is a corresponding growth in organisational participation, strength, and political consciousness among broad layers of the wider membership.

Therefore, a key question for the left to confront when key positions in unions are won is whether or not the victory is built on the back of rising member activity, class consciousness and combativity. It is important to acknowledge that many left leaders elected over the past decade or so have secured victory on very small electoral turnouts, while many union executive positions are elected uncontested.

This dilemma is true at local levels, too. Many left activists are not elected to key roles such as branch secretary positions on the high tide of class struggle and consciousness, but rather an ebb tide of low levels of organisation and engagement. Holding these positions, which again are often uncontested, necessitates doing the routinised work of individual representation, consultation and negotiations with employers – often around 'defensive' issues such as restructurings and redundancies. These 'trade union duties' will often be carried out on 'facilities time' (sometimes full-time facilities time), resulting in both a potential divorce from the workplace and little time available to build union strength and capacity. Even the most committed activists can find themselves drawn into an individualised model of 'heroic leadership', where the officer solves problems and issues *on behalf of* colleagues, as opposed to building collective leadership where issues are resolved collectively. The pressure towards this individualised model of leadership, with its tendency to demand more and more time from a small number of activists, also has wider consequences for union-building. For example, in the NUT (and still in the NEU), women make up 76% of workplace reps (reflecting the proportion of women members in the union), but only make up 40% of local secretaries. As long as women continue to disproportionately undertake domestic labour and caring roles, there will continue to be structural obstacles to their full participation in trade union activity.

This is not to argue that individual representation is unimportant, nor is it to argue that all individual issues can be collectivised, rather it is to highlight a tendency of behaviour. This tendency towards the 'bureaucra-tisation of the rank and file' is by no means inevitable, but it is a very real danger. It therefore must be underlined that this critique is not a moral judgement whereby left activists are seen to be failing in their radical duties, rather it is to acknowledge a situation born out of the material realities of working-class defeat and retreat and a corresponding decline in trade union organisational coherence and strength. This reality cannot be denied, and needs to be grappled with. There may be no easy or guar-anteed answers, but reality does need to be confronted. Only then does it become possible to sketch a roadmap ahead.

Finally, while accepting that elected left leaders, at a national and local level, are important, but not enough to renew the movement in and of themselves, what left leaders *do* in the current context to build power and organisational strength *does* matter. Indeed, the relationships and inter-actions between left full-time officials and rank-and-file activists and members are crucial in the context we find ourselves in.

The starting point here is to underline that although subject to the same disciplines of the workplace, not all workers, or union members, share the same understanding, have the same motivation, or share a con-sistent set of politics. This is especially true in the era of low levels of collective struggle and organisation. The development of class conscious-ness and combativity are complex processes that can often change quickly and dramatically in unexpected ways. This contradictory consciousness results from the interaction of multiple objective and subjective factors both within the workplace and in wider society. So while understanding that sustainable and effective renewal will come only through high levels of activity from rank-and-file activists and members in the workplace, it is simply not good enough to say the answer today is to 'build the rank and file' without understanding how this is to be achieved in concrete terms in the context of at least four decades of generalised defeat and retreat – not only from class struggle in general, but also seeing unions as vehicles of collective class organisation that can secure real and meaning-ful change at work and in society. If exhortations were a viable route to renewal, renewal would already have occurred!

It is therefore not satisfactory to say that 'the bureaucracy' has been responsible for 'holding back' the rank and file, and if only 'the leader-ship' would call strike action, then this would see an upsurge in struggle. The experiences documented in this book shows that calling action can result in upsurges of activity, but not always, and these upsurges are only built and sustained through a unity of interests among members, a clear goal and target, and a conscious intervention to build grassroots organisation. Detailed effort needs to be committed to genuinely supporting members' self-organisation, and not just following national or local calls to mobilise around this or that issue. This is not to dispute that even left full-time officials, because of their employment status and the sometimes contradictory pressures inherent in their social position, have directed struggle to seemingly pragmatic rather than more radical ends, nor is it to say the actions of union leaders in giving a national lead are unimportant, but it is to argue that confined to the level of dogmatic sloganeering, this position offers neither a satisfactory explanation of the current context nor a credible practical road map to renewal.

It is in the context of this analysis that we provide an overview of the dominant responses in the trade union movement to the crisis of organised labour.

RESPONSES TO RETREAT: SOCIAL PARTNERSHIP AND 'INSTITUTIONAL ORGANISING'

The first decade of the Conservative government could best be described as a classic 'war of movement' against the organised labour movement. The 1984–1985 miners' strike was the stand-out conflict of the time, with the state's resources mobilised on an unprecedented scale to ensure victory, but the decade also saw high-profile disputes involving steel workers, nurses, printers and, in turn, teachers. The impact on the labour movement was evident over the decade as both union membership and 'days lost' due to strike action began to plummet. It was not until the 1990s that it became possible to identify clear strategic responses to these developments, presented here as social partnership, and institutional organising. In describing these approaches, they may at first sight appear as binary opposites, but we argue the two strategies had more in common than might appear to be the case initially, and hence were able to co-exist within TUC strategy.

Social Partnership

With the big battalions of the labour movement defeated, pessimism about the possibility of resisting the Thatcherite narrative that 'there is no alternative' to neoliberalism took hold in the upper echelons of many trade unions. Rather than looking at ways to rebuild the collective activity and strength of members to counter the increasingly marginalised role of organised labour in industry and society, solutions were looked for elsewhere. One such solution was set out in a speech made to the Trades Union Congress in 1988 by Jacques Delors, then President of the European Commission. Delors offered an apparently enticing vision of enshrined sectoral collective bargaining, job protection and trade union rights across the European Union.

The concept of social partnership was embraced by many in the trade union movement desperate to reclaim a seat at the negotiating table that Thatcherite approaches to industrial relations were denying them.[11] As part of this strategy, greater emphasis was placed on the individual services and benefits trade union membership could bring to workers (sometimes referred to as 'service model unionism'). John Monks, elected General Secretary of the TUC in 1993, pursued this strategy further, going so far as establishing a 'Partnership Institute' in 2001.

Advocates of such an approach argued that partnership would lead to mutual benefits (a so-called 'win–win' model) and greater trade union 'voice' in workplace matters, and would thus improve trade union effectiveness. However, arguably the outstanding feature throughout the long rule of the Conservative Party at this time is that there was little or no national-level political impetus towards employers and employees being considered as potential 'partners' working to secure an agreed way forward on industrial matters. Starting from a position of labour movement weakness, no legislative framework was developed to facilitate social partnership. Indeed, in terms of legislation, the decades of neoliberal advance after the election of the Thatcher government witnessed further legal constraints on trade unions that undermined their legitimacy as actors within industrial, economic and political matters. As John Kelly (1996, p. 88) noted presciently, 'it is difficult, if not impossible, [for unions] to achieve partnership with a party who would prefer that you didn't exist'.

Significantly for the purpose of our analysis, it is important to note that arguably the most high-profile example of social partnership in the UK was established in the school sector in England and Wales between 2003 and 2010 (during a period of Labour government). In this instance, it arose as a response to the unusual co-operation of teacher unions using the threat of united action to secure a reduction of teachers' workload. The education unions (representing both teachers and support staff), local authority employers and central government formed an ongoing institutional arrangement to secure agreement on a number of reforms known as 'workforce remodelling'. The arrangement was always contentious (the NUT never joined the Social Partnership, while one of the headteachers' unions joined, left, rejoined, and was then excluded) and is associated with a range of controversial workforce reforms (such as the use of cover supervisors to manage whole classes). The threat of conflict succeeded only in the unions being incorporated into an employer agenda. With the unions divided and disorganised by the strategy, the arrangement was immediately abolished when the New Labour government was defeated in 2010 and the Conservative-Liberal Democrat coalition took power.

Institutional Organising

In what may appear as a contradictory move, at the same time as the TUC was promoting partnership working it also began to advocate for an approach based on workplace organising titled 'New Unionism' (represented most conspicuously by the establishment of the TUC Organising Academy in 1998). The apparent contradiction was reflected in organising's traditional location in the conflict paradigm within industrial relations, in which employer and employee interests are considered inimical and beyond being reconciled. By definition, this contrasts sharply with any notion of 'partnership'. Edmund Heery (2002) summarised the organising approach as follows:

> the 'empowerment' of workers, in the sense of stimulating activism and strengthening trade unionism in the workplace in order that workers can resolve their own problems without recourse to external representation. Membership, it is believed, is best built and sustained by effective workplace organisation.
>
> (p. 21)

Beyond this analysis, however, it is widely acknowledged that the actual practice of institutional organising in the UK often has little conceptual clarity or consistent application within and between unions. Jane Holgate (2021) has argued that the term is sometimes used as a catch-all to cover any activity that seeks to connect with workers at their workplace, often with no more ambition than the recruitment of new members. Quite commonly, 'organising' is defined more by what it *is not* (it is not social partnership, and it is not 'servicing') rather than what it *is*. As a result, there is a real danger that many of the key elements of organising as a means to build union power through democratic worker self-organisation that directly challenge managerial authority at the frontier of control are lost in a lazy invocation of a bland commitment to 'member engagement'. Indeed, this is why we argue that the TUC's simultaneous commitment to both partnership and institutional organising was not at all contradictory if organising was conceived in very narrow terms, with a focus on recruiting members in order to enhance credibility in partnership deals (or, after the election of the New Labour government in 1997, winning formal union recognition by demonstrating a majority commitment to union recognition among workers in any given 'bargaining unit').

The high hopes of promised renewal through institutional organising soon gave way to first caution, and then pessimism, under evaluation of its application. Indeed, some seven years after the launch of 'New Unionism', some argued that the term 'organising' had become meaningless and simply acted as:

> a rhetorical device that ... enables oligarchic forces to sustain the current forms of governance, goals, and methods of unions. ... A genuine grassroots organising model does not need modelling; it is, by definition, simply something that people do *without* top-down influence.
>
> (de Turberville, 2004, p. 788)

Although we share concerns that 'organising' in its application is uneven and risks being mobilised as a strategy of organisational management – what Mel Simms (2007) and others have called 'managed activism' – rather than as part of a political struggle that challenges the power of employers and the state, we do not share de Turbeville's wider conclusions. The utility of 'organising' is that it starts from the position of divergent interests between employers and workers. The analysis presented by de Turbeville also fails to reflect the complexities of how leadership is enacted in trade union organisations, and by whom. The utility of the 'organising model' is precisely in the potential it affords to theorise the nature of the relationships between material conditions, the political consciousness of workers, and the influence of leadership and leaders.

Notwithstanding concerns about the malleability of the concept – indeed, perhaps precisely because of its status as 'all things to all people' – there is no doubt that 'institutional organising' developed as an easy-to-support orthodoxy in the trade union movement throughout the 2000s. Hence, by the late 2010s this orthodoxy, even in its uneven application, often existed more at a rhetorical level than in reality, as shown, for example, by the TUC's winding up of its Organising Academy in 2019. Institutional organising, while doing some good in focusing, to an extent at least, on union members and union growth, had not provided the panacea to renewal.

However, what has become clear is that as the commitment to institutional organising has become more ambiguous, the interest in organising approaches among grassroots activists has continued to grow. Much of the credit for this development can be attributed to the work of Jane McAlevey and the linked 'Organising for Power' project,[12] which looks at drawing and generalising lessons from successful trade union organising actions, where the question of building trade union power is front and centre.

McAlevey's work claims to draw on the organising tradition of the US Congress of Industrial Organizations trade union confederation in the 1930s, which at the time was known for its effective methodical approach to rank-and-file organising of industrial and agricultural workers. McAlevey's contemporary reworking of this approach in her book *No Shortcuts* (2016) is framed around five core concepts, presented as a set of binary propositions. First is the concept of the 'structure' as the basic unit of organising. For McAlevey, 'structure' refers to the boundary around a pre-formed unit in which members share common interests, but not common views, values or opinions (this contrasts with 'self-selecting' groupings, such as single-issue campaigns, where members choose to join on the basis of a shared commitment). Second, McAlevey highlights the importance of 'organic leaders' she deliberately counterposes to 'activists'. The latter are important, but are frequently not sufficient. Leaders are those workers with significant credibility across the workforce, and therefore with the ability to influence those indifferent, or quite likely hostile, to union organisation and action. Leaders often have a track record of informal worker organising, but this may well be completely outside the union. Leaders themselves may be hostile to the union initially, and winning them to the union becomes a key task. The focus on leaders' ability to shift the thinking of 'hard to reach' workers highlights the importance of McAlevey's third concept – the need for majorities (in contrast to actions based on a minority of the workforce). McAlevey's argument is that worker power derives from workers taking action together, and that this links directly to the proportion of workers involved. Action is effective when a significant proportion (what McAlevey calls a 'super majority') of the workforce are involved. This is a powerful argument, although it arguably gives limited space to those cases where a minority of activists have been successful in their disputes because the impact of their action has been strategically important.[13] McAlevey's fourth key concept is 'whole worker organising', by which she is referring to the way in which effective trade union actions have been able to amplify their power through genuine, organic, coalitions with communities. Again, for McAlevey this is achieved through worker self-organising in communities and an authentic integration of worker and community interests. It stands in contradistinction to a contrived suturing together of loosely linked issues in order to co-opt community support for pre-defined union demands, forming what McAlevey (2016, p. 207) calls 'slick (but shallow) community-labor alliances'. McAlevey's final concept is that of organising itself, which is presented in opposition to 'mobilising'. Organising's power analysis is rooted in the conflict paradigm, and is committed to worker self-organising building super majorities in actions that challenge the frontier of control. In contrast, mobilising is grounded in the pluralist paradigm, and tends to be determined by union staff (or 'activists' in the McAleveyian sense). It is driven from above and outside, and typically fails to reach beyond the minority of those already committed to the union. McAlevey argues that it often depends on burning out activists and relies too much on messaging and framing (increasingly communicated through social media) to compensate for structural weaknesses.

A great strength of McAlevey's work derives from the way in which she has connected her ideas with those engaged in labour and community struggles to provide practical support for union and community organising. The appetite for this type of support is reflected in the extraordinarily high levels of participation in the 'Organising for Power' programme, with online courses engaging cohorts of thousands from around the world. In particular, the work has provided a great service by emphasising workplace-based organising (the centrality of the 'structure'), recognising the role of leaders(hip) and relentlessly focusing on the need to build broad support across the workforce. We particularly value McAlevey's challenge to all those in the labour movement to reach out to, and connect with, those who do not typically participate in formal union structures but without whom collective action struggles to break through.

However, the absolutely understandable commitment to have a ready answer to activists who ask 'What is to be done?' also risks reducing complex contexts to a formulaic response. The attraction of a 'how to ...' guide has an obvious appeal to union activists frustrated by the failure of their efforts to yield progress and who often have little or no experience of what winning looks like. However, the promotion of a model in the form presented by McAlevey can be problematic if it appears to suggest a 'one best way' of organising (a notion reinforced by McAlevey's own references to 'the science of effective struggle': 2020, p. 204). Furthermore, the inextricably linked assumption is that it is professional organisers who know and understand the model ('the science') and whose role it is to bring this understanding to the workers. Ironically, therefore, and counter-intuitively given the associated claims, Moody (2020) argues that 'the "model" preserves or even enhances a dominant place for the professional organizer' based on the assumption that the organizer 'knows' and their task is to transmit their knowledge to those who do not know.

In *No Shortcuts*, Jane McAlevey presents four detailed case studies of this type of renewal, with one of the cases focusing on the experience of the Chicago Teachers' Union (CTU), whose strikes in 2012 have provided inspiration to trade unionists within and beyond education. The CTU strike was significant because it marked a moment when years of union compromise and declining influence were halted, and indeed reversed. Hence the interest it has generated across the USA, and beyond. This was the point at which the NUT began to develop a direct link with the CTU leadership, inviting them to present at an international conference on the Global Education 'Reform' Movement in 2014, sending activists to Chicago to study with them, and engaging in a number of bilateral discussions, including two CTU leaders attending and addressing the NUT Annual Conference. In this way, the experience of the CTU had a direct and significant impact on renewal discussions within the NUT.

The CTU strikes followed years of defunding in Chicago's public schools, combined with a programme of public school closures and charter school openings that disproportionately impacted Chicago's urban Black and Brown communities. Indeed, highlighting the racialised, and racist, elements of education policy in the city was to be a key element of the campaign to resist the closure of valued community schools. Resentment was building both within the affected communities and in the public school workforce, but the CTU leadership before the strikes was unable to channel, or perhaps even recognise, this anger. As a result of this inertia within the organisation, teachers began to self-organise inside the union, forming a left opposition caucus – the Caucus of Rank and File Educators (CORE). Simultaneously, they began to reach out to community organisations that were challenging the school closure programme. In due course, the established leadership was overturned in an election in which supporters of CORE won every seat. Significant in all these developments was the role played by women and Black leaders in the union, most obviously the CTU President, Karen Lewis.

The campaigning within the CTU culminated in nine days of strike action in September 2012 when the union not only secured the over-whelming support of the union's membership, but also won high levels of popular support in the community, and despite all the efforts of the city mayor to fracture this alliance, the coalition of union and community held together and was key to securing the strike's victory. In understanding the success of the CTU strike, which has directly influenced education union organising across the USA, it is possible to identify several key factors that contributed to the achievement. It has already been mentioned that CORE took seriously the need to win community support, and brought this approach into the union leadership when its members ran for election. This proved to be pivotal. Several studies of the CTU strikes have demonstrated how union activists worked patiently and respect-fully with community activists, carefully avoiding being seen to 'take over' existing community campaigns or cynically co-opting community support for union campaigns. Trust was built, and solidarity developed, through patient collaboration around issues of central concern to the community. In a country where some previous disputes had highlighted serious tensions between teacher unions taking action and the Black and Brown communities affected, this trust-building was critical.[14]

This support was further developed by the union's framing of its own demands within a broad bargaining agenda that focused on linking the quality of the learning environment with decent working conditions. This approach was encapsulated in the slogan to be found at CTU picket lines and rallies – 'teachers' working conditions are our students' learning conditions'. A significant step forward in this regard was the development of a campaigning document, *The Schools Chicago Students Deserve*,[15] that set out a clear, well-researched and articulate prospectus for change that provided dissatisfied students, parents and educators with a clear critique of the *status quo* and a set of demands that provided an alternative. The union had its own 'story' which connected with the aspirations of students and parents and challenged the logic of the system reformers. McAlevey (2016, p. 124) quotes an activist who argued that the work allowed people to 'imagine a different type of Chicago'.

Alongside all this outward-facing work with community activists and organisations, the new union leadership worked assiduously to connect with members in schools, making sure the union had a presence in every workplace and that members in schools understood and felt they 'owned' the union's demands. A number of 'structure tests'[16] were deployed, such as surveys and mock strike votes, that both raised member awareness and tested members' understanding of the issues and their commitment. At each stage, data were analysed forensically to both ascertain overall levels of support and identify particular areas of strength and weakness in specific schools. Where support appeared less strong, appropriate remedial action could be taken (rather than the situation being ignored). Throughout the process, the new leadership made efforts to open up the bargaining process by encouraging members to draft bargaining demands and ensuring that negotiations were reported faithfully with decisions on outcomes subject to full debate and democratic decision-making.

As indicated, the success of the 2012 CTU strikes has had considerable impact in the USA and elsewhere (not least because nothing inspires and builds confidence more than winning). One obvious manifestation of this was the extraordinary #RedforEd teacher strikes that took place in several Republican-governed states starting in spring 2018 (Blanc, 2019). The first strike took place in West Virginia (Republican-controlled, but with a history of labour organising linked to mining), and strikes quickly followed elsewhere (often in states with very little tradition of union organising). These states typically had no collective bargaining arrangements, and in some cases strikes were illegal. Despite these constraints (or perhaps because of them), a combination of years of defunding (hitting both working and learning conditions), associated frustrations and the emergence of new grassroots activists intent on challenging the *status quo* resulted in a wave of strike action in the most unlikely places, but also often highly successful. What Casey (2020) calls the 'Teacher Spring' in the red states in 2018 fanned out to both Republican and Democratic states over the next 12–18 months, forming what Casey refers to as a 'teacher insurgency'. One element of this teacher insurgency was the 2019 Los Angeles teachers strike in which 34,000 members of the United Teachers of Los Angeles (UTLA) voted 98% in favour of strike action on an 84% turnout. In this dispute, the UTLA took six days of strike action and won a contract that included key working conditions issues, but also a range of other issues, including guaranteeing green spaces and access to public parks for local children. The campaign also built strong alliances with Los Angeles' largely Hispanic public school community. Jane McAlevey analyses the UTLA strike in her more recent book *A Collective Bargain* (2020), and identifies several factors as crucial to its success, including a change in local leadership and an ability to win community support by framing the dispute as a campaign for the future of public education in Los Angeles. This was crucial to winning the public support that created the political pressure that won the dispute.

However, McAlevey is also clear that the success of the campaign depended on the new union leadership bringing in three full-time organisers with a history of building and winning industrial disputes. These organisers set about building member commitment by making sure members in every school (900 schools) were visited, propagandising around the union's demands and putting in place multiple structure tests to build, and gauge, the member commitment and support that was central to success.

Unambiguously, but arguably controversially, McAlevey (2020) states:

This can't be emphasised enough: *the teachers sought full-time union staff who had successful strike experience* ... there hadn't been a teachers' strike in LA since 1989 – so how would the rank and file teachers know how to get strike ready?

(p. 205; emphasis in original)

There is no question that stories of the teacher strikes in the USA, from Chicago to Los Angeles, via West Virginia, Kentucky and elsewhere, are an inspiration (see also earlier work by Lois Weiner, 2012). There is much to learn from what happened, and is happening, in the USA, and it is good to see how connections have been made between activists and academics, often across borders, in order to draw out the lessons. In this volume, we seek to contribute to this collective learning process by analysing the specific experience of the NEU/NUT and its own 'turn to organising' in a context that has many similarities, but also important differences, with the US examples. In the next section, we begin this analysis by identifying how the NUT's 'organising in practice' was in turn shaped by research and theory.

THE NEU/NUT 'TURN TO ORGANISING': CONNECTING THEORY AND PRACTICE

The NUT could not in any sense be described as in the vanguard of the trade union movement's turn to institutional organising, in part because its relatively high density insulated it from the pressures for change experienced by many other unions. Arguably, it was not until ten years after the TUC established the Organising Academy that any such committed 'turn' can be identified (when in 2008 the NUT appointed its first Organising Academy trainees). This, it should be clearly noted, is not to say that before this turn members and activists were not already systematically trying to build union power, but it is to note that this experience was not generalised – or institutionalised – enough to halt the slow creep of atrophy of some local structures, as internal research commissioned by the NUT and conducted by the Labour Research Department had demonstrated.

Any change in an organisation as complex and diverse as a large trade union is inevitably difficult, but especially so when the change is substantial in both structural and cultural terms. A number of political visions compete for influence, particularly among the activist base, and the relative strength of these is in turn linked to the organisational capacity of different groups and factions in the union (formal and informal). In addition to the influence of lay members, union officials have significant interests in shaping organisational responses, and as with the lay activist base, union officials will have diverse interests and views.

It is not our intention in this volume to provide a detailed sociological study of the NUT's 'turn to organising'. We make no effort to map the personalities, the internal political positions and the events that can help explain this shift, as it is beyond the scope of what we aim to achieve. Rather, what we intend to do is show how a range of theories and ideas were being engaged with, by activists and officers, as the union sought to both give direction to, and embed, its commitment to organising. In this chapter, we identify three separate frameworks that can each be linked to the development of the NUT's organising agenda. We recognise that such an approach can appear to impose a tidiness on what we acknowledge is a complex, indeed messy, process. However, we also want to argue that these frameworks helped inform and underpin the *institutional* shift in the NUT's strategic direction.

The three approaches are Peter Fairbrother's work on union responses to fragmentation and New Public Management (1996), including his work on union democracy (1984); the research undertaken by Bob Carter, Howard Stevenson and Rowena Passy (2010) on workforce remodelling and the strategic choices facing education unions; and finally, John Kelly's (1998) use and development of mobilisation theory to seek to understand when, and under what circumstances, workers collectivise and resist. We argue that each of these separate pieces of work had an identifiable influence on shaping the NUT's organising agenda, and when taken together, may be considered to offer an albeit loose theoretical framework for analysing developments in the union.

Peter Fairbrother's research in the 1990s was concerned with how the introduction of New Public Management into the civil service was impacting on the work of civil servants and also the response of their trade unions. His work highlighted the need for trade unions to analyse the context in which they were working and be willing to respond and adapt to changed circumstances. New Public Management was just such a development: a class-based strategy intended to create a hostile environment for trade union organisation by decentralising operational decision-making to workplace level, thereby fracturing the traditional structures of solidaristic trade union organisation. The key frontier of control, between employers and trade unions, shifted more obviously to the workplace, and pitted local management against individual employees. Fairbrother recognised all the attendant problems this (intentionally) posed for trade unions, but argued that the same developments that were seen as threats to trade unions also presented opportunities. His argument was that the essential conflict between employer and employee, which had historically been deliberately drawn away from the workplace in order to absorb and accommodate it, was increasingly being played out in the workplace. No longer were issues being resolved by complex negotiations, using procedures many workers did not understand and conducted by people they did not know, but rather the frontier of control between themselves and management was directly in front of them and visible. It was Fairbrother's contention that this had the potential to generate collective responses from workers, and that this in turn offered the possibility of developing a more active and participatory form of trade unionism:

> With moves towards more decentralised forms of management, union members have taken tentative steps to generate participative and active forms of unionism ... where union members exploit these structural circumstances, there is the prospect union renewal will occur.
>
> (1996, p. 111)

For Fairbrother, the key to union renewal was the extent to which it deepened democracy in the union and opened up spaces for member participation, which he argued took three forms: first, an integration of representation and mobilisation (so that workplace representatives are the organic link to member mobilisations); second, high levels of member involvement in decision-making ('this means that local members can and do take decisions on issues and topics which directly concern their immediate work and employment relations'; Fairbrother, 1996, p. 113); and third, a reorganisation of democratic structures to maximise the opportunities for member involvement in decision-making, in particular the members' meeting which Fairbrother described as the 'leitmotif of union activity' (1996, p. 113).

At the time, Fairbrother's conclusion was that evidence pointed to renewal as both embryonic and uncertain, with much hinging on whether trade unions made strategic choices to respond bureaucratically or democratically. The former would suffocate renewal, but the latter could deepen it.

Many of these issues were developed in the specific context of the education sector in the research undertaken by Carter and colleagues in 2010. Their study focused on the impact of the workforce remodelling agenda (and therefore the Social Partnership) on industrial relations in the English school sector during the period of the New Labour government.

Their approach started from an analysis of the impact of the workforce reform agenda on the labour process of teaching, and identified how Taylorist principles of scientific management (Taylor, 1911/2004) were being applied to teaching (increased managerialism, greater task specification, more measurement of performance). The research also highlighted how a new division of labour was emerging in schools, with a growing gap between those undertaking what official policy documents called the 'core task of teaching and learning' and those engaged in roles supporting teaching. In this way, the academic and pastoral elements of teaching were increasingly separated, with the responsibility for 'caring' being allocated to a largely female workforce (working on poorly paid, and frequently term time-only, contracts). All of these developments served to reinforce the structural inequalities built into the education workforce in which those already experiencing most discrimination in the labour market (women, Black workers, the disabled) had their experiences compounded by low pay and insecure contracts.

At this time, New Labour's education policy was driven by a crude subordination of the education system to the demands of the economy and the imperative to develop human capital. This inevitably had a huge impact on teachers and teachers' work, combining an intensification of teachers' labour with a loss of job control. Under these circumstances, it would have been reasonable to expect a collective response to develop that challenged the increase in such pressures, in particular from the NUT, which had opposed key elements of the remodelling agenda and therefore sat outside the Social Partnership. As it was, such a response proved difficult to mobilise and was largely conspicuous by its absence. There is no doubt that this can be partly explained by the divisions between teacher unions, meaning that any form of collective action could not win support across the whole workforce. However, it almost certainly also reflected the decline in the NUT's organisational strength as the increasingly fragmented school system exposed underlying weaknesses in the organisation, including a lack of workplace representatives. There were sporadic and isolated efforts to challenge the use of those without a teaching qualification to take responsibility for whole classes, but such action was difficult to mobilise and proved impossible to sustain. On this single issue – the use of those without teaching qualifications to take on teacher roles, a defining issue for the NUT – the union was unable to mobilise an effective campaign of opposition.

In their analysis, Carter and colleagues identified three strategic responses available to education trade unions as they confronted the neoliberal restructuring of state education. We introduced these responses in Chapter 1 as Carter and colleagues' (2010) framework of *rapprochement*, resistance and renewal. *Rapprochement* was presented as an approach that fundamentally accepts the prevailing system and seeks to work within 'the rules of the game'. It is not the task of the union to provide a fundamental challenge to the dominant system, but rather the purpose of the union is to secure the best available deal for members *within* the system. The *rapprochement* approach does not rule out conflict, including the taking of strike action, but conflict is not seen as systemic, but rather the sign of a system that has broken down. During the period of Carter and colleagues' research, the Social Partnership offered an obvious example of *rapprochement,* as the model was premised on going with the grain of New Labour's education reforms. However, despite the NUT's opposition to Social Partnership and workforce remodelling, the approach can also be used to describe much of the NUT's strategy in the post-war period when the welfare state was expanding and the union enjoyed close relationships with local and national government.

In contrast, the strategy of resistance stands in opposition to the neoliberal restructuring of state education. At times, there may be pragmatic compromises, but in principle, the strategy of resistance is based on recognising the fundamental antagonism between employer and employee, and organising to challenge this. It recognises that union power resides in the mobilisation of workers in collective actions. Resistance therefore described union efforts to challenge neoliberal attacks on working conditions and trade union organisation, but it did so in an essentially reactive and negative manner, without sufficient alternative vision of the relationship between aims and forms of organisation: union organisation itself was fundamentally unaltered. Drawing on McAlevey's analysis, it was often activist-led and organisationally top-down, relying on grassroots members to step up, or step down, as required. The union's repertoire of actions was often limited. In theory, it relied on strikes to support collective bargaining when negotiations appeared to falter, but in reality, as collective bargaining arrangements were progressively undermined, traditional strategies of resistance proved insufficient to defend them. It appeared to work well when levels of member commitment were high and members could be relied on to support calls for action. However, where member commitment was low, for whatever reason, trade unions seemed unable to mobilise members to even defend current rights. We do not wish to caricature, but the danger of the resistance strategy was that it had no strategy for building union power beyond an exhortation to 'struggle harder'.

Recognising that *rapprochement* was unacceptable, and resistance on its own was not sufficient, Carter and colleagues argued that renewal involved linking necessary strategies of resistance with organisational reform of the union itself in a way that focused relentlessly on the active building of union power. Renewal therefore comprised many elements, including the deepening of union democracy, a focus on workplace organisation, a reculturing of the organisation to ensure the full participation of women, Black, disabled and LGBT+ members, and a strong focus on member education and activist development. It also recognised that none of these transformations could take place without a focus on teachers and others contesting not only terms and conditions, but also the labour process of teaching in its widest sense, including issues such as the control of the curriculum, pedagogical and professional autonomy, and the abolition of standardised tests. This emphasis entailed linking the commitment to good educational practice to the interests of pupils and their communities. Trade unionism had to re-establish its relevance to the everyday practice of teachers, rather than being synonymous with national leaders and annual pay claims. However, in making the case for renewal, limited detail was provided about its form, and in many ways it has been left to unions to construct this detail *post hoc*. In this book, we seek to overcome this limitation, and take the work of Carter and others forward, by providing a case study of union renewal in practice that can help fill out some of the detail missing from the original analysis.

The third area of work that the NUT drew on as it developed its organising strategy was that of mobilisation theory. Mobilisation theory has been developed within the sociology of social movements, and has sought to understand the circumstances in which individuals organise collectively and take action to bring about change. In a trade union context, it was developed in particular by John Kelly (1998), who used mobilisation theory to explain the circumstances in which workers take action together. At the centre of Kelly's use of mobilisation theory is the concept of *interests* (aspects which advantage or benefit someone). When interests are threatened, there is the possibility that a sense of injustice develops.

In a work context, the threat to interests is likely to relate to control of the labour process, but the notion of injustice can be experienced more widely over any relevant issue. What is key is that a sense of injustice is experienced, as it is the basis for collective action. However, a sense of injustice on its own does not guarantee a collective response, and several other factors need to be taken into account. For example, Kelly highlights the importance of *attribution* – the need for workers to be able to identify a person or body responsible for their grievance, combined with a conviction that those responsible can address the problem if pressured to do so. Within mobilisation theory, the concept of *organisation* occupies a central position, referring to the extent to which potential participants in an action identify themselves as social actors sharing a common interest. Put simply: is the sense of injustice a shared understanding, and is that shared interest recognised as such? Does the group with the grievance have a collective identity?

Where there is a shared sense of injustice, combined with a belief that those responsible can be compelled to address the issues if subject to sufficient pressure, then there is a basis for a potential collective mobilisation. However, Kelly's use of mobilisation theory also draws on a number of other issues to help identify the circumstances in which the collective action is actually realised. Many of these factors hinge on the type of action available to those involved and their assessments of the chances of success. Mobilisation theory reminds us that there are costs of taking action (loss of pay in a strike, possible victimisation and reprisals) and that those participating in the action make assessments of the costs and benefits when making decisions about whether or not to commit to action. There are also other factors that can impact this calculation (union density levels, assessments of whether fellow workers will commit to the action), and these too form part of the decision as to whether to mobilise or not.

Finally, Kelly highlights as a crucial factor in this decision the role played by local leaders. These he describes as that 'small but critical mass of activists' whose role involves 'promoting a sense of grievance' by challenging accepted inequalities and creating or sustaining 'a high degree of group cohesion' (1998, p. 127). This critical focus on leaders as a key element of mobilisation theory had implications for the way the NUT developed its organising approach.

The utility of mobilisation theory for the NUT was its ability to help understand the dynamics of collective action in the much-changed circumstances of an increasingly fragmented system. Whatever collective action had looked like in the past, it was clear that the much-changed landscape in the English school system required a different focus and approach. It was not that national action across a fragmented system was not possible, but that it needed to be built in a different way. This required much more focus on actively building at the base of the organisation. It also recognised that the trigger for such collective action was often an injustice specific to a particular workplace, resulting from systemic factors, but often arising from how these were experienced in the very specific circumstances of an individual workplace. Building union power involved identifying the issues that confronted members, and then developing the sense of collective identity to give members the confidence to tackle them for themselves. This became the basis of the union's commitment to issues-based workplace organising. It was also the foundational building block for developing a commitment among members to a model of active trade unionism.

Kelly's development of mobilisation theory in an industrial relations context has enormous value when seeking to understand the dynamics of collective action, but it is important to recognise that it is a theory which can help to understand; it is not a formula that can be used to predict. All of the factors that are brought together within mobilisation theory and that can help understand whether mobilisations are possible are the product of how workers *make sense* of their context. In this book, we identify this sense-making as an important element of consciousness. Two workers confronted by exactly the same working conditions do not necessarily experience the same sense of injustice. One may see no injustice, or may feel a sense of injustice, but believe it is the outcome of a set of circumstances beyond their control. They may attribute the injustice to their own personal failings – 'I have a problem with my workload, but it is my fault because I am not sufficiently resilient.' All of these outcomes are possible, and collective action will only develop if the sense of injustice is understood and shared, and if workers believe that taking collective action can tackle the injustice. Developing this shared understanding of the problem, its causes and how to confront and tackle the problem is about shifting consciousness. It is a process that always starts from workers' immediate concerns, the problem that confronts them in their work and which is the basis for their potential sense of injustice, and which turns frustration into action. It is always an active process, and those engaged in it are acting as leaders, although often not in any formal sense. Thinking of leaders in this way then helps us to reframe leadership in terms of the broader function rather than the formal role. These are issues we will develop further in the following chapters.

In setting out these ideas, we are not suggesting that the NUT's 'turn to organising' was based on a conscious effort to meld together a range of theoretical approaches, any more than it was a search for an 'off-the-shelf' solution or a pre-formed blueprint. Rather, we are claiming that there were serious efforts to connect theory and practice in a genuinely dialectical process. Ideas had to be applied in the very specific circumstances of a rapidly changing English school system and tested in the crucible of practice. The works presented above helped the NUT develop and cohere its organising strategy as it sought to rebuild union power in the face of structural reforms intended to deal a fatal blow to trade union organisation. However, the union's experience as it has developed its own road to renewal has also highlighted where the union (now a larger organisation representing a more diverse workforce of teachers and support staff) and the wider labour movement need to do more work. In the following chapters, we seek to make our own contribution to these debates, not least by exploring in more detail what we understand by 'leadership' in the context of the labour movement. In many senses, as Stevenson (2016) has argued, leadership can be considered the missing link, not just in mobilisation theory, but across all the ideas presented here. Moreover, while we acknowledge the absolutely central role of organising in the renewal of the NEU/NUT and its focus on building union power, we also argue that the story of the NEU/NUT points to the development of an expanded conception of organising and to the need to go 'beyond organising' in any narrow sense.

3

Class Wars: Public Education and the War on Teachers

As the Second World War came to an end and the defeat of fascism was in sight, the contours of Britain's post-war welfare state began to emerge. What followed were significant advances in the fields of heath care, social security and public housing, together with a commitment to full employment. One of the earliest manifestations of the new welfarism and the 'spirit of '45'[1] was in the area of education policy, where commitments to expand secondary schooling, and a raft of associated reforms, placed education at the heart of the post-war welfare state. All of these developments represented major gains for the working class. Nevertheless, it is important to understand the post-war welfare state as the outcome of a class compromise in which the interests of both labour and capital were temporarily reconciled around a particular settlement that sought to offer both groups tangible gains. For sure, the welfare state significantly enhanced the quality of life for large sections of the working class, but the state's intervention in the areas of welfare provision, public ownership of key industries and macroeconomic policy was also designed to stabilise the economic environment and create the conditions for further capital accumulation. It simultaneously compensated for the chronic failures of the free market system that had been exposed in the pre-war years, while also winning the support of a working class made angry by years of depression and war. Underpinning this delicate equilibrium of class forces was the emergence of Keynesianism as a new economic orthodoxy apparently capable of sustaining growth and full employment through the technocratic management of demand in the economy.

The Education Act 1944 was a consummate reflection of the welfare state compromise. It expanded free secondary education, and included several other important advances for the working class. But it also established a tripartite model of secondary education based on the creation of grammar, technical and secondary modern schools. The model reflected traditional notions of 'fixed intelligence' that had long been reflected in state education policy, and which were used to justify directing particular students to particular school types, and from there into particular forms of work. The legislation also consolidated the influence of Church organisations in the public system, while leaving Britain's elite private schools (confusingly referred to as 'public schools' in the UK) untouched. As such, the 1944 Act firmly reproduced and entrenched the class-divided nature of the English social system. The 1944 settlement also retained the key role of local authorities as the managers of local school systems, thereby ensuring a significant element of democratic community control.[2]

In the years after the war, the urge for further social progress soon became evident as frustration with the divisive, and clearly class-biased, model of tripartite schooling began to grow. This emerged most explicitly in movements for non-selective forms of education (comprehensive schools) and the related shifts in pedagogical practices to ensure young people received a genuine comprehensive education *within* schools as well as rejecting selection *between* schools. This move took a major step forward in 1965 when the Labour government encouraged local education authorities to adopt plans to develop comprehensive schools in their areas. Although some local authorities resisted, it was clear that a decisive moment had been reached.

The experience of comprehensive school reorganisation was always uneven and often contested (sometimes from within the teaching profession). However, it is also important to understand that the progress being made was about much more than a system reorganisation. Rather, it was underpinned by significant curricular and pedagogical innovation. Teachers were developing new child-centred pedagogies (a phrase now frequently misrepresented and caricatured) that challenged the fixed-ability thinking that reproduced social division. Much of this work was supported by the growing influence of education departments in universities, and was given a significant boost by publication of the Plowden Report in 1967.[3] The report asserted that 'at the heart of the educational process lies the child' and contributed to 'a perceived revolution in primary school practice' (in Lowe, 2007, p. 46). It was also driven by primary school teachers, who were able to capitalise on the significant amount of autonomy afforded within the English school system and often supported by local authorities whose networks of teachers' centres (run by teachers for teachers) created spaces for teachers to collaborate on curriculum innovation and pedagogical practice. The educational historian and campaigner for comprehensive education Brian Simon (1991) described this period as the years of 'break out' for progressive education.

We do not seek to oversimplify developments at this time, because they were clearly uneven, but what was emerging was a new democratic professionalism in which an increasingly well-qualified profession had both the organisational frameworks to collaborate with others, and the institutional spaces to innovate and exercise professional judgement. This created conditions in which teachers, working together, could craft the curriculum, and their pedagogy, in ways that started from the needs of the child. Children were not expected to fit to a school system that did not recognise their world, but rather teachers had the space to start from the experiences of the children, in all their richness and diversity.

What quickly became apparent was that as the move towards the type of education we have described above built among teachers, parents and in wider civil society, the forces of reaction and resistance began to mobilise. The earliest signs of the ideological challenge to welfarism can be traced back to the year of the Education Act 1944 and Frederick Hayek's critique of collectivism in *The Road to Serfdom* (1944/2001). This spawned an international network of neoliberal think tanks based mostly in the United States, but also in the United Kingdom. Education was always a central concern of these groups because they recognised the vital ideological function performed by education as well as the critical role it played in the (re)production of labour. Hayek's influence on education reform became particularly apparent in Chile, where the Pinochet dictatorship (with direct links between Hayek and Pinochet) rapidly introduced a radical programme of school privatisations.[4]

In the UK, and specifically England, this ideological challenge to the left's advances emerged in 1969 when the opening number of a series of Black Papers was published in the journal *Critical Quarterly*. The first of the papers was significantly titled *The Fight for Education* (Cox and Dyson, 1969), and set out the contributors' opposition to what was presented as a dangerous trend towards egalitarianism in education policy, most clearly expressed by the developments in primary school education, but also in universities, where the impact of the 1968 student protests was still reverberating. What is perhaps most significant about the Black Papers is that the attack on progressive education was rooted in a defence of traditional notions of 'Britishness': class, family, order and deference. As such, the Black Papers reflected the cultural basis of much of the right's critique of education policy, anticipating the enduring influence of neo-conservatism within neoliberal Conservative Party education policy since that time. They serve to remind us that there is nothing new about what today are referred to as 'culture wars', but rather these are merely the latest iteration of an ongoing ideological struggle about what it means to be a citizen (or in the UK, a subject).

By the end of the 1960s, it was clear that although the movement for a more egalitarian education system was gaining momentum, the political right was already organising to take back control. In the 'fight for education', forces were being marshalled and the battle lines were being drawn.

ECONOMIC CRISIS AND THE END OF WELFARISM

The struggle for comprehensive education continued to make progress into the 1970s, not least during the period when Margaret Thatcher was Secretary of State for Education and Science. However, the ideological struggle over the future direction of the education system could not be disconnected from the economic crisis that was also unfolding at the same time. As post-war welfare states had expanded, this placed pressure on capital's ability to accumulate, hence the drive at the time to both contain public spending and to weaken the power of organised labour. An early sign of the developing tensions was evident in 1969, when members of the NUT and National Association of Schoolmasters undertook the first ever national teachers' strike in England and Wales. The dispute was eventually settled in 1970 (the same year the NUT became a member of the Trades Union Congress), with the NUT executive committee claiming 'a substantial victory for the Union and a complete vindication of its policy of militant action' (Seifert, 1987, p. 103).

As it transpired, the 1969 teachers' strike presaged a decade of skirmishes between teachers and the state (both centrally and locally) as the developing fiscal crisis sharpened tensions over first pay, but later public sector spending cuts, school closures and teacher redundancies. Indeed, it can perhaps be argued that this period was a 'coming of age' for the teacher trade union movement as it mobilised industrially on a national scale and teacher trade union organisations discovered the power of their collective strength.

Like other sectors of the economy, this was also the period when left-wing rank-and-file organisation and activity developed considerably in the union. In the NUT, this was represented by two competing, often conflicting, strands. One saw the growing influence of sections of the Labour left and the Communist Party, while the other saw the increasing importance of the Rank and File caucus that had been established in 1967 (mostly by activists in the International Socialists, and later the Socialist Workers' Party). As the union's membership shifted to the left, the union engaged in a wider range of struggles beyond those narrowly focused on pay and conditions. Local union branches often played a key role in anti-cuts campaigns, while there was also increased activity in relation to anti-racist education and wider anti-fascist struggles. This was reflected in the work of, among others, the All London Teachers Against Racism and Fascism (ALTARF),[5] but was also illustrated by the murder of NUT member Blair Peach by the police at an anti-fascist demonstration in Southall in 1979 (Renton, 2014). In many cases, such activity by local associations set up tensions between local activists and members of the NUT's national executive, most obviously in London, where the Inner London Teachers' Association organised local industrial action in defiance of the national executive. As a consequence of these developments, the union's 1973 annual conference introduced a new rule that prevented local associations from calling industrial action without prior national executive agreement. In so doing, it highlighted the uneasy relationship that often existed in the union between local associations and the national leadership.

These internal tensions around union strategy would play out again as the union confronted not just issues of pay and jobs, but also the far more fundamental question of teacher independence and autonomy, which increasingly became matters of public and political debate. This became evident when a dispute about so-called progressive teaching methods erupted at William Tyndale School in North London in 1974,[6] which was quickly followed by a 'Great Debate' about education launched by Prime Minister James Callaghan. At the core of Callaghan's argument was that the English education system was failing to equip students for the labour market, or put another way, failing to provide capital with the labour required to generate capital accumulation. Teachers' autonomy in relation to determining pedagogy and curriculum was implicitly identified as the problem.

What was becoming increasingly apparent was that the 'fight for education', originally identified by the Black Paperites, was about more than defeating militant teachers striking for better pay; the real fight was over the curriculum, and by implication, the wider purposes of education. As the economic crisis intensified, there is no doubt that education policy increasingly focused on the vocational purposes of education, underpinned by a commitment to human capital theory (HCT). This was the logic of the so-called 'Great Debate', or 'great betrayal', as Clyde Chitty (1993) called it. Associated with the work of Gary Becker (1962), HCT asserted that economic success required workers to possess the necessary skills and capabilities to maximise productivity, assuming a straightforward, and indeed causal, linkage between levels of investment in training and skills development and the level of returns to capital. This has always been a central purpose of education policy, but began to assume increasing importance as economic problems accelerated and global capitalist competition intensified. However, education policy in England has also always been about much more than a simple focus on human capital development, so demands to subordinate educational objectives to the demands of the economy also had to be reconciled with policies intended to strengthen traditional notions of class, nation and family.

These struggles over the purposes of education have emerged as conflicts over the curriculum and are realised in practice as struggles over teachers' work – what teachers teach, how they teach it and who gets to decide the answers to these questions. This is why struggles over teachers' work can never be restricted to narrow questions of pay and workload, but must always address the totality of teachers' work. In this analysis, there can be no distinction between so-called 'industrial' and 'professional' issues. It is all work, and every issue is a potential union issue.

THATCHERISM AND EDUCATION: THE NEW RIGHT ON THE OFFENSIVE

In spring 1979, following the so-called 'Winter of Discontent' in which many local campaigns had mobilised teachers to oppose education cuts and redundancies, Margaret Thatcher was elected as the new Prime Minister. It marked the end of the post-war settlement between the state, capital and labour, and was part of a global rebalancing of class forces in favour of employer interests. One obvious sign of this new era was marked by the UK state's willingness to confront organised labour, often in those areas where trade unions had been traditionally strongest. This approach, that we describe as a war of movement in the Gramscian sense, was intended to 'confront, defeat and destroy' the power of organised labour. It was deployed most visibly in the dispute with the National Union of Mineworkers in 1984/1985, when the vast resources of the state were mobilised to inflict a defeat on the union that continues to have consequences for the trade union movement nearly four decades later.

During this time, and rather overshadowed by the miners' strike, teacher unions found themselves in a dispute over pay with their local government employers that lasted for two years (involving strikes and actions short of strikes, such as working to contract) (Rieser, 2016). Although pay was the headline question, the conflict arguably reflected a wider set of issues that stretched back to William Tyndale and the 'Great Debate', and which revolved around questions of job control and teacher autonomy. *The Times* newspaper recognised the issues and commented in an editorial at the time that 'the dispute is about management, not money' (in Ball, 1988, p. 290) – framing the war on teachers, starkly and accurately, as a battle for the control of teachers' work.

The dispute was both long and complex. The centre of negotiations was the national collective bargaining machinery that had been established in 1919, known as the Burnham Committee. On the trade union side, the National Union of Teachers had a majority on the Burnham Committee, but co-ordinating the industrial action in a multi-union environment involved intricate intra-organisational bargaining between different unions. On the employers' side, the situation was no less complex, with the local government group balancing both Labour and Conservative representatives, and central government also having a decisive influence. Although local authorities were technically the employers of teachers, the bulk of the finance was provided by the central state, and over several years the Department for Education and Science had been able to assert ever greater control over Burnham negotiations (including a secret deal in 1965 that substantially increased its voting power on the Burnham Committee) (Seifert, 1987). In a period when a key government objective was to drive down public expenditure, it was inevitable that central government was likely to use all its influence to impact the outcome of negotiations.

After two years of what had seemed like a long war of attrition, the dispute ended with a settlement between unions and employers (brokered through the state's arbitration service). The outcome was presented as a compromise between employers and unions, but at the time it was widely regarded as a defeat for the trade unions, which had struggled to maintain much more than a fragile unity throughout the campaign. What had started as a dispute over pay produced an outcome that tied pay reform to conditions of service. The new contract specified teachers' working hours (1,265 hours per year, allocated over 195 days) and created the conditions for the increased managerial control of teachers' work. The final deal fell far short of the unions' objectives during their members' two-year campaign (Rieser, 2016), and also represented a decisive shift in the balance of power in favour of the employers. During much of the dispute, teachers had demonstrated great discipline and resolve, co-ordinating action at school level, but by the end of the dispute, teachers were exhausted, divided and demoralised.

It is hard to overstate the importance of the 1984–1986 teachers' action. Sadly, its political and historical significance remains largely ignored, being overshadowed, understandably, at the time by the miners' strike. However, it would be a mistake to underestimate its significance, because the central state's strategy was in many ways the same for teachers, as it was for the miners – to take on a strategically important section of the trade union movement (in this case, the new militants of the white-collar public sector) and to seek to 'confront, defeat and destroy'. This was a consummate 'war of movement' in the Gramscian sense, in which the state mobilised in a direct attack against a group of workers whose ideological function and importance made a confrontation inevitable.

Shortly after the dispute ended in 1987, the Conservative education minister unilaterally declared that the Burnham Committee was to be suspended and presented the outcomes of the negotiations to parliament in the form of a Statutory Instrument (thereby replacing a collective agreement with statutory imposition). The government then replaced the Burnham Committee with an Interim Advisory Committee (IAC) of 'independent experts' that would make recommendations to the government on teachers' pay. Trade unions (and local authority employers) could provide evidence to the IAC, and the government would then accept or reject the IAC's recommendations. However, there was to be no formal negotiating in any traditional sense. Both of the major trade unions, the NUT and National Association of Schoolmasters/Union of Women Teachers (NASUWT), responded to this development with strike action, but industrial action was difficult to deliver given teachers' recent experiences of action, and their subsequent fatigue. As divisions opened up in the teacher trade union movement, the Conservative government subsequently made the interim arrangement permanent and replaced the IAC by the School Teachers' Review Body (STRB). It is therefore the case that school teachers in England have not been able to engage in national collective bargaining in relation to their members' pay since 1987.

The second dramatic development in the aftermath of the 1984–1986 industrial action was the passing of the Education Reform Act 1988. This represented one of the most substantial and significant interventions by the central state in education since the 1944 Act, and its impact was to completely up-end the post-1944 system and set the English school system on an entirely different trajectory. The legislation was the coming together of a number of ideas that had been developing in New Right think tanks for several years, which, when cohered into an integrated whole, would fundamentally reorientate English schooling as a system based on market principles.

The legislation contained several major reforms, each one of which represented significant structural change. First, the legislation introduced a statutory national curriculum for 5–16-year-olds into a system that had historically had very high levels of professional autonomy. Student achievement in this curriculum would then be measured through new standardised national tests for 7-, 11- and 14-year-olds, alongside the existing assessment of 16-year-olds. The purpose of the new standard-isation (reinforced through published league tables of test results) was to provide parents, now cast as 'consumers', with information to make choices about their child's school. This 'parental choice' (more apparent than real) was made possible by a system of so-called 'open enrolment' contained within the Act. Alongside these reforms, local education authorities were required to devolve much more of their education budget directly to schools, with the money allocated according to 'pupil units', thus ensuring that the money schools received was very directly linked to the number of pupils they enrolled. Headteachers and governing bodies were then given much greater flexibility about how they chose to deploy their budget (Local Management of Schools), and were able to decide, for example, whether to spend money on staff or equipment. Schools that wanted even more autonomy could 'opt out' of local authority control completely (subject to a ballot of parents) and become 'grant-maintained' (GM), whereby they received all their funding directly from government. GM schools had the power to determine their own pay and conditions for staff.

In many senses, the 1988 Act captured the (often uneasy) equilibrium between neoliberalism and neoconservatism in Tory education policy. Much of the emphasis on marketisation was intended to create a dynamic competitiveness between schools while also opening the school system up to new forms of privatisation. Curriculum reforms similarly reflected these tensions, with a skills-based vocationalism[7] jostling for curriculum space with a knowledge-based traditionalism. All of this in turn was underpinned by a relentless attack on ground-breaking curriculum developments in anti-sexist and anti-racist education that had been driven by progressive local authorities such as the Inner London Education Authority (ILEA), but also in Manchester, Sheffield and elsewhere. These attacks included introducing the notorious 'Section 28' legislation that made it illegal for local authorities (and by implication, schools) to 'promote' homosexuality.[8]

To a young teacher in England today, who not only works in the system we are describing but may well have been schooled in it, the reforms of 1988 may seem historically distant and remote (although they are no longer constrained by Section 28, which was repealed in 2002). This is an analysis and history that is no longer widely debated. For example, it has been largely expunged from increasingly standardised teacher education programmes as the state has intervened in determining the content of teacher training. It is not a history that elite groups want education workers to know and understand.

However, they will almost certainly recognise how the key elements of the 1988 system shape and define their work today. Reconfiguring state schools in England as autonomous business units immediately put pressure on those managing the system (headteachers of 'autonomous schools') to get 'more for less' from their staff. Competition between schools generated pressure to demand more and more 'output' – now evaluated by the standardised tests that made it easier to measure, compare and rank (between schools, but also between teachers), while devolved budgeting allowed and encouraged managers to drive down the costs of labour (by, for example, recruiting teachers at lower points on the pay spine or replacing qualified staff with staff who had fewer qualifications). This relentless drive to push output up while simultaneously driving costs down in turn required a more forensic focus on the work of individual teachers and their performance. Standardised testing led inevitably to standardised teaching, and a trend, still prevalent, to adopt some 'one best way' model of teaching. All of these trends were then encouraged or penalised, as appropriate, using the new appraisal- and performance-related pay systems that followed shortly after 1988.

The structural changes introduced into the post-1988 education system have resulted in the systematic intensification and deskilling of teachers' labour. The result today is that teachers in England work longer hours than teachers almost anywhere else in the world, and the chronic recruitment and retention crisis experienced in England is a direct consequence of the structural pressures caused by the drive to both control and intensify teachers' labour. There can be no understanding of today's school system, and the impacts it has on students' experiences and teachers' work, without understanding the 1988 reforms. The reforms intentionally injected a substantial measure of 'market discipline' into the English school system, with attendant consequences for those who study and work in it. The educational consequences of the marketisation of schooling quickly became evident as the introduction of league tables led to sharp rises in pupil exclusions (hugely impacting the experience of Black and working-class young people). So-called 'system gaming' (covertly selecting or excluding students to manipulate league table performance) rapidly became commonplace, and since then league tables and high-stakes accountability have intensified gaming on an almost industrial scale (again, with Black and working-class students disproportionately impacted, an outcome even more pronounced in academy schools). Education inequalities have widened as educational experiences have narrowed. It is the children in working-class schools who perform least well, but who experience the exam factory culture at it sharpest.[9] The failure, after decades of inaction, to tackle the disproportionate exclusion of Black students from mainstream schools continues to attest to the structural racism in education that the 1988 Act intentionally reinforced.

However, our argument is that to focus only on educational outcomes is to misunderstand other important objectives of the Education Reform Act 1988. There can be no doubt that one of the key aims of the 1988 reforms was to break up the public education system in England and make it much easier for private capital to enter the lucrative education 'market'. Private interests are now represented in the English public education system in multiple, complex and often opaque ways (contracting out of 'back office' services, extensive use of private consultancies etc.). However, it is important to recognise that one of the key purposes of the 1988 Act was to introduce market forces into the education system as a disciplinary mechanism to create a more conforming and compliant workforce, prevented from mobilising resistance to government policy by the divisive and destabilising effects of competition. Abolishing national collective bargaining, undermining the power base of teacher unions at local authority level and subjecting individual schools to the pressures of competition were all intended to deal a fatal blow to teacher trade union organisation. Moreover, as if this was not enough, in 1992 the government established Ofsted as a hugely powerful centralised inspectorate whose judgements on individual schools would have profound effects should a school be judged as 'failing'. In this way, Ofsted added a state-driven managerialism to the 1988 Act's marketisation, and the two elements have combined to create a pincer movement of control, enforcing compliance through downward competition and a culture of fear. The point was well illustrated by a headteacher interviewed shortly after the introduction of Ofsted:

> Basically, in the run-up to Ofsted my authority as the headteacher was paramount. When you compare that with the teachers' [industrial] action, I wasn't running the school – the NUT were.[10]

In the war on teachers, the right were taking back control.

NEW LABOUR: NEW PARTNERSHIPS

The election of a Labour government with a landslide victory after 18 years of Tory administrations was met with considerable optimism by many working in education, particularly as Labour leader Tony Blair had signalled that education was the party's key priority (or famously, the party's top three priorities – 'Education, education, education'). However, it quickly became apparent that the years of New Labour government would present education workers with a very mixed picture, because although investment levels in education increased, and there were undoubtedly some sound individual policies (such as the abolition of grant-maintained schools and of the Assisted Places Scheme, which had acted as a state subsidy to private schools), there were also many issues that proved problematic for teachers.

Labour's education policy agenda during the Blair years was dominated by the focus on developing human capital and aligning educational purposes to the needs of the economy and capital. This was made clear by Tony Blair's speech to the 2005 Labour Party conference:

> education is our best economic policy …. This country will succeed or fail on the basis of how it changes itself and gears up to this new economy, based on knowledge. Education therefore is now the centre of economic policy making for the future. What I am saying is, we know what works within our education system, we can learn the lessons of it. The key is now to apply those lessons, push them right throughout the education system, until the young children … wherever they are, they get the chance to make the most of their God given potential. It is the only vision, in my view, that will work in the 21st century.
>
> (in Ball, 2013, p. 12)

Here, Blair makes explicit that education is key to securing competitive advantage in the globalised capitalist economy and that education policy is one element – indeed, *the* element – of an economic policy focused on capital accumulation. In this sense, Blair's commitment is no more than a continuation of Labour policy extending back as far as Callaghan's 'Great Debate' 30 years earlier. What was also significant was Blair's claim that 'we know what works' (foreshadowing a key motif of Michael Gove's later intervention in education), and therefore the only challenge was to 'push' the policies 'throughout the education system'. Teachers experienced this 'push' most obviously as 'national strategies' for literacy and numeracy, whereby teachers came under enormous pressure to not only deliver specified content, but to deliver it in very specific ways. The national strategies, and a raft of linked reforms, inevitably had an impact on teachers' workloads, but the more significant impact was on the content of teachers' work and the ability of teachers to make professional decisions, based on an assessment of the needs of pupils, about what to teach and how to teach it. In many senses, teachers' experiences at this time represented classic 'Taylorism', with moves towards a further division of labour (through the expansion of the role of teaching assistants – without commensurate pay), standardisation and imposition of a 'one best way' model of working on teachers. These changes again highlighted the importance to teachers' perceptions of themselves as 'professionals' and the reality of their diminishing control over their own labour process. This new Taylorist scientific management was to be implemented through the creation of a new managerial class, trained at the newly created National College for School Leadership (established in 2002), and buttressed by appraisal systems and performance-related pay (significantly enhanced in 1998). As ever, Ofsted remained the back-up to ensure compliance, although the inspectorate's powers were now enhanced by rigorous school-by-school target-setting and public 'naming and shaming' of so-called 'poor performers' (almost always schools serving the most deprived communities).

From the outset, teacher unions resisted the dramatic increases in workload that flowed from New Labour's so-called 'standards agenda'. Education unions commenced industrial action on workload issues, with the action co-ordinated across all major unions. This display of unity was illustrated in 2001, when all three major teacher unions passed an identical motion calling for a 35-hour week at their annual conferences. As a direct result of such pressure, and the growing problems caused by industrial action, central government, local authority employers and trade unions began discussions aimed at addressing the workload problems in schools. Although not a formal negotiating mechanism, the talks represented the first meaningful discussions of this type between government, employers and unions since the abolition of the Burnham Committee. The outcome was a national agreement officially titled *Raising Standards and Tackling Workload: A National Agreement* (usually referred to as 'the workload agreement'),[11] in which a number of measures were identified, some substantial, intended to reduce teachers' workload problems. At the time, the NUT stood out against the agreement because one of its provisions allowed for teaching assistants to cover the classes of absent teachers in order to reduce the amount of 'covers' (lesson substitutions) that teachers might have to undertake. For the NUT, this violated the principle that every class should be taught by a fully qualified classroom teacher, which was a campaigning principle that had long defined the union's commitment to an all-graduate and appropriately qualified profession. The NUT therefore refused to sign the workload agreement, and consequently ruled itself out of the 'Social Partnership' that had developed the agreement and that became formalised and ongoing after the workload agreement was signed off.

The years of Social Partnership (2003–2010) were therefore – somewhat ironically, given the name – fractious years in the profession, as the Social Partnership unions by and large worked closely with the Labour government and developed an ambitious 'workforce remodelling agenda', while the NUT sat outside these discussions and tried to navigate a path of opposing key reforms while also having to live with their implementation (which, as a union working on its own, it struggled to prevent). As it transpired, the divisions relating to the Social Partnership were resolved without union intervention as the new Coalition government elected in 2010 immediately abandoned the arrangement and hence eliminated the division between those within, and without, the partnership.[12]

The New Labour years were unquestionably very different to those of the previous Conservative government, with the state mobilised in particular ways to drive forward education reform. However, despite very significant differences, there was also much that was common. Although Labour quickly abolished grant-maintained schools, it was soon clear that there was no commitment to row back from the marketisation of the school system that had been set in motion in 1988. On the contrary, New Labour intensified competitive pressures in the system by ratcheting up the accountability mechanisms and adopting a punitive approach to those schools deemed to be 'failing'. Much of this approach was accompanied by a 'reculturing' of the system through newly established 'academy schools' (in essence, grant-maintained schools reinvented) and 'Education Action Zones', both used to break up established local authority systems and create a more 'dynamic' school environment in which the new cadre of school managers (now rebranded as 'school leaders') would be less constrained and more 'entrepreneurial'. In essence, the school system continued to be reconfigured in ways that undermined traditional public service values and sought to mimic private sector practices.

In many senses, this period effectively marked a new phase in the struggle for control of teachers' work. If organised teachers were perhaps not seen as the enemy, they were certainly seen as the problem. In this sense, the Social Partnership (which the Labour government only established after initial reluctance) can be seen as a consummate compromise between a state requiring teacher support to deliver its reform agenda and a teaching profession that still bore the scars of its 1980s defeats and which had failed to rebuild after that period. As discussed in Chapter 2, this was a period of *rapprochement*.

What was clear was that although New Labour interrupted many aspects of the Thatcherite agenda in education, it by no means disrupted the wider project. Indeed, almost all the key elements of the 1988 architecture (centralised curricula, standardised testing, open enrolment, devolved management and budgeting, and a version of 'independent state schools' – i.e., academies) were either reinforced or remained completely unscathed, ready and waiting for a new right-wing government to pick up and push on from where it had left off in 1997.

THE NEW RIGHT RETURNS: AUSTERITY AND THE ONGOING ASSAULT ON ORGANISED TEACHERS

The UK general election of 2010, following on from the 2008 economic crisis, resulted in Labour's defeat and the election of a coalition government of Conservatives and Liberal Democrats. Significantly, the education portfolio in Cabinet was allocated to a senior figure from the right of the Conservative Party, Michael Gove, illustrating how the organised right has always understood the strategic ideological importance of education. Very quickly, it emerged that the Tory Party saw education policy as a key area for radical reform, with its white paper *The Importance of Teaching*[13] signalling an overhaul of almost every aspect of the school system, including teacher education, curriculum and assessment, school governance and accountability, and school funding mechanisms. No aspect of the system was to avoid 'reform', and it was clear that the Thatcherite revolution in education that commenced in earnest in 1988 was firmly back on track. This resumption of hostilities had been clearly trailed prior to the election by Tory Party leader David Cameron in an interview in the *Daily Telegraph* in February 2009:

> The structural change is we've got to bust open the state monopoly on education and allow new schools to be established. It's what's happened in Sweden, in parts of America it's hugely successful in terms of making sure there's excellence, there's competition, there's innovation and new excellent schools come along. It's a big chance. It will mean some big battles with forces of resistance. Some LEAs might not like it, some of the education establishment won't like it.

There are forces in the education establishment that have to be taken on and defeated on this.[14]

This was the 'fight for education' that the Black Papers had demanded more than 40 years previously, and which had been waged as a war on teachers ever since, but which was now emerging in more explicit form. The Tory Party was at war with the 'education establishment', which needed to be 'taken on and defeated'. The language is important. These are their words.

One of the early signs of conflict was the national public-sector strikes over pension cuts in 2011, in which education unions played a prominent role (including the first national strike action by the Association of Teachers and Lecturers). The action involved 2,000,000 public-sector workers and secured some modest concessions. However, cross-union unity in the wider trade union movement soon fractured, and the biggest UK strike in decades failed to develop into a broader movement to challenge austerity. It was also apparent that the attacks on education workers were not only about austerity, but reflected a more deep-rooted ideological challenge. This emerged in two forms, once again suturing together the right's neoliberal and neoconservative elements to develop an education agenda that was simultaneously radical and reactionary.

The right's neoliberal instincts were most clearly reflected in the commitment to encourage all primary and secondary schools to become 'academies' (the revised version of grant-maintained schools that New Labour had established). The intention was to establish every school in the country as a stand-alone business unit managing its own budget and with the 'freedom' to determine its own terms of conditions for employees. Parallel to this development, and acting as a key impetus to 'academise', was the experience of local authorities that were reeling under the impact of austerity policies imposed on them by central government. One obvious consequence was that local authorities slashed the services and support they provided to their schools, but in more extreme examples, it positively encouraged some of them to 'offload' their schools to become academies as they sought to scale back their own responsibilities.[15]

For the Tories, the drive to academise helped to break up the local authority-based school system and to make the system more 'private-like', if not fully privatised (because the production of human capital is far too important to be left to the free market!). It certainly allowed for more private-sector involvement (through more contracting out of services), but it also encouraged schools to mimic private businesses functioning in a competitive market. Crucially, it created a hostile environment for trade union organisation. Not only did it dismantle many local authority-based bargaining systems, with their associated local agreements and support for local union officers (facilities agreements), but it also reduced trade union organisation to organising in often small workplaces and competitive, isolated environments. The drive to break up the public education system in England and to establish a fractured and fragmented (non-)system of academy schools is a deliberate class strategy, operationalised through the state, that seeks to fundamentally weaken the power of organised teachers. This has been a war on teachers, and it has been relentless.

Parallel to the drive to academisation and the deepening of market mechanisms in the system was a commitment to a fundamental overhaul of both the curriculum and teaching that placed education at the centre of a neoconservative cultural revolution. Drawing again on Antonio Gramsci, this was to be the latest phase in the right's long war of position against the 'progressive' teaching methods and curriculum innovations that were the scourge of the Black Paperites. An early sign of the new conservatism in the classroom was the imposition of a phonics-based approach to literacy, but this was soon followed by a much more substantial drive across the whole system to restructure the curriculum around so-called 'core knowledge'. There is not the space in this volume to provide a detailed critique of this approach, but its consequence has been to promote a very specific, culturally biased curriculum in the name of giving all children access to 'the best that has been thought and said' (a phrase associated with the 19th-century headmaster of Rugby School, Thomas Arnold, that is quoted directly in the 2014 English National Curriculum framework). The roots of this approach to the curriculum can be traced to the USA, where the academic E. D. Hirsch (1999) first articulated the ideas. At first appearance, it can seem difficult to challenge (because to oppose it can appear as though one is opposing access to, and the acquisition of, knowledge itself), but the reality is that what is considered 'the best that has been thought and said' is what has been decided by an elite within society who are interested in reproducing, not transforming, the social system. At the same time, the drive for 'core knowledge' (a Hirschian phrase also used in official National Curriculum documents) cannot be separated from linked commitments to 'direct instruction' as the preferred pedagogical approach and the use of so-called 'zero-toler-ance' behaviour policies in schools. These developments are inevitably presented as politically neutral and guided by a commitment to make the best available to all. The reality is that this is a profoundly political agenda (a form of Black Papers 2.0) in which knowledge is defined, gen-erated and delivered by an elite, with those who resist rejected by the education system (zero tolerance) to be managed by an equally uncom-promising criminal justice system. The rhetoric of 'social mobility' masks a project committed to reasserting conservative notions of Englishness and imposing on working-class and Black communities a new culture of conformity and compliance (Reay, 2017). Those who seek to give young people the conceptual and thinking tools to question this new social order find themselves harangued by government ministers who, for example, challenge the teaching of critical race theory on the spurious grounds of 'balance'.[16] These attacks are no different in essence to the Thatcherite attacks on anti-racist education projects in the 1980s. Structural racism is deeply embedded in the educational system, which is precisely why gov-ernment ministers do not want teachers to be able to discuss these issues with their students.

Driving forward with this neolib-neocon/radical-reactionary agenda in education has presaged new strategies and tactics in the war on teachers and the struggles over teachers' work. It has simultaneously involved a direct confrontation with those David Cameron pejoratively described as 'the education establishment' (and whom Michael Gove portrayed as 'the Blob'[17]), while also constructing a new education establishment of its own supporters and allies. In this process of dismantling and reconstruction, the right has identified three principal targets: local authorities, univer-sity education departments and education trade unions. Local authorities were to be undermined by academisation and removing them from any meaningful role in the management of schools. This process would be accelerated by austerity, which disproportionately shifted the cost of cuts from central to local government and decimated local authorities' abili-ties to provide support to schools. At the same time, university education departments (held responsible for promoting pedagogical approaches that conflicted with what government ministers wanted) were to be increas-ingly sidelined in teacher education by shifting responsibility for teacher training into schools. Teacher training was to be focused on meeting the expectations of a system driven by the Ofsted inspectorate, rather than equipping future teachers with the knowledge and understanding to be critical and reflective professionals working in a system riddled with structural inequalities. As we write, the latest iteration of these developments is a reform of teacher training which sees a new body (the Institute of Teaching) established to give the central state even greater control over how teachers are trained. The clear intention is to expunge independent critical perspectives from the system and to ensure future teachers are trained in the system, by the system ('by schools for schools', according to the DfE[18]). This is how reproductive systems work.

Meanwhile, and all the time, the government has had the teacher unions in its sights. The attacks on teacher unions were in part to be achieved through the promotion of academies and the corresponding downgrading of the role of local authorities. This threatened to dismantle the local authority structures where unions remained relatively strong, while replacing this with a fragmented environment intentionally difficult for union organisation. However, as identified in Chapter 1, the government also sought its own direct confrontation with education unions, and in 2012 the government briefed sympathetic media sources that it was preparing for a major confrontation with education unions over performance-related pay and that the Department for Education had been placed on a 'war footing'. As it was, the teacher unions were able to undermine the proposed pay reforms without engaging in the direct confrontation the government was clearly trying to engineer. However, efforts to undermine the teacher unions continued relentlessly, not least in the following year, when the Secretary of State for Education enthusiastically supported the launch of an organisation specifically set up as an alternative to trade unions. Edapt was, perhaps significantly, established by an ex-Teach First teacher (an English-based version of the Teach For America model) as a subscription-based service for individual employees experiencing problems at work. It continues to be very small, and remains largely irrelevant, but its presence as part of the right's new educational landscape remains significant. Following its launch, the Secretary of State for Education stated:

> Now there is no need for teachers to feel they have to join a union if they want full employment protection – they can get impartial legal and employment advice from an organisation without a political

agenda. And it is great that this organisation is teacher-created, teacher-designed and teacher-led.[19]

This is a hegemonic project *through*, and *within*, education. It is a hegemonic project *through* education because the political right have long recognised the need to win popular support for the basic tenets of neoliberalism. Education performs a vital ideological function in society by forming individuals both as workers and citizens. Education equips workers with the skills that capital requires but it also shapes identities to (re-)produce 'responsible' citizens and idealised national identities. Understanding this social order as natural, and as the widely internalised 'common sense' of the day, is a key part of the ideological function of education. It is precisely why the right have made the curriculum such a battleground, because they understand its central role in shaping future citizens. However, this project of constructing a hegemonic consensus *through* education (at least in part) can only be achieved by also securing a hegemonic consensus *within* education. By this we mean the right's efforts to embed their mix of neoliberalism and neoconservatism as the new common sense among those who study and work in the education system. This is why the right have been so determined to dismantle what they refer to as the 'education establishment', and replace it with *their* education establishment that goes far beyond an alliance of its own neoliberal and neoconservative wings, but includes the school leaders, the new teacher training providers, the think tanks and the social media personalities who now play a key role in embedding the Tory's brand of radical reaction as the established common sense in education policy.

While much of the detail may be specific to English education, this is an approach to education reform that has travelled globally, not least because many of the organisations that promote these agendas are global corporations with interests in many different countries.

This has also been a successful project in many respects. Years of restructuring have transformed the English education system. The radical potential of the post-war years has been halted, and a very different education system has been developed. The resources of the state have been mobilised to secure these objectives (from the use of a bloated but hugely powerful inspectorate to reinforce government objectives through to the reform of teacher training to promote particular state-endorsed approaches to pedagogy), and it is inevitable that the new 'common sense' has become, to some extent, internalised.

That said, if what is being described represents a revolution, then it is vital to acknowledge that it has only ever been partial and incomplete, and that in this moment, as we live in a time of perpetual crises, it is vulnerable.

The reality is that the drive to restructure public education in England has always been contested, and fundamental elements of the reforms have always been challenged. Standardised testing, for example, has always been opposed by large sections of the workforce in schools, and this shows no signs of abating. Similarly, the drive to academisation has been challenged by many campaigns opposing the transfer of a local school to academy status, and the system more widely continues to be the subject of ongoing critique. Much less visible, but no less important, are the countless ways education workers find to push back against government policy in their own classrooms (Marks, Cox and Little, 2022). If it is a revolution, then it is what Antonio Gramsci described as a 'passive revolution' that has been driven by a powerful state, but which has shallow foundations at the base.

Perhaps the clearest example of the failure of the project has been the failure to defeat the teaching profession itself, and specifically the organisations that represent education workers' collective interests – their unions. Despite all the efforts to 'confront, defeat and destroy', not only do teachers remain highly unionised, but there is increasing union density among education support staff, and increasing unity between support staff and teachers (formalised when the National Union of Teachers and the Association of Teachers and Lecturers amalgamated to form the National Education Union as the largest education union in Europe). This is a unity which will be essential in halting and reversing the impact of the political right's war on teaching.

4

Building Power in the Workplace

If you can organise my school, you can organise anywhere.

(NUT school representative[1])

The Education Reform Act 1988 introduced dramatic changes to the English school system. It deliberately created a quasi-market of competing schools, ranked in league tables of test scores, one aspect of which was the delegation of a raft of personnel responsibilities to school level. Collective agreements that had been negotiated at local authority level between employers and unions no longer applied, but rather school governing bodies were charged with the responsibility for deciding their own policies. Previous local authority-level policies for dealing with redundancy, staff discipline, grievance and capability became the responsibility of school governors, while policies relating to the observation of teaching and the management of performance also became school-level issues.

The most obvious impact of these developments appeared to be on the work of the school union representative (the 'school rep'), as this was the person who now represented the union at the point where key decisions were to be made. However, the problem facing the unions was that the 'school rep' had historically been a relatively weak link in the union organisation. This was in large part because school reps typically had an ambiguous role. All schools with union members were expected to elect a representative, but the reality was that many, even most, schools did not have a rep, and where they did, the reps were not necessarily expected to *do* very much. The limited nature of the role was reflected in their original title – *school correspondent*. School correspondents were expected to distribute the union journal in staff rooms and put union communications into members' pigeon holes (methods of communication that are now largely irrelevant). If problems developed at school level, some reps might try to resolve these issues themselves, but more commonly they would pass the issue upwards to the local association secretary. Many school reps had been explicitly recruited on the basis that they would not have to undertake any activity much beyond this minimal list of responsibilities, and indeed sometimes local union officers actively discouraged reps from doing so, for fear of reps 'getting it wrong' (reported in the research by Carter, Stevenson and Passy, 2010). There was little expectation that the school rep would act as a *bona fide* workplace bargainer, seeking to negotiate with the headteacher over substantive issues (see Stevenson, 2001 and 2005).

The reforms of 1988 were intended to fragment the system, and to undermine the role of both local authorities and local authority-based trade union organisation. As such, they posed a major threat to which the union needed to respond. At a bureaucratic level, the NUT acted by establishing new regional structures that were intended to devolve union resources in a way that reflected the new school system. However, related reforms, proposing a review of the roles of the school rep and the local association, met considerable opposition from local activists who feared efforts to marginalise the role of the local association. In the context of a deeply divided union, with low levels of organisational trust between activists and leading officials, the proposals were seen in some quarters as the latest iteration of a strategy intended to weaken local associations at the expense of the organisational centre. Responses to the consultation paper[2] that set out these reforms were very largely negative, and at the NUT's 1993 Annual Conference the National Executive report indicated it was not intending to pursue the proposed reforms, but would keep the situation 'under review'.

With hindsight, this was probably a key moment when the union needed to face up to the profound changes reshaping the English school system, but when it failed to do so. NUT influence was predicated on participation in national collective bargaining and being firmly embedded in local authority industrial relations systems. Within a few short years after the end of the 1984–1986 industrial action, neither of these pillars of influence existed in anything like the form they had done before the dispute. What was required at the time was a serious analysis of the new landscape, its implications for the union, and a strategy for maintaining union power in these changed circumstances. However, what emerged was a much more pragmatic approach. Rather than seize the opportunity to renew, the union reconciled its instincts for both *rapprochement* and resistance in efforts to 'hold the line' and to try to build back the local authority structures that the 1988 Act was intended to dismantle.

Such an approach had obvious attractions, not least because it appeared to be effective. The NUT and other education unions, often working with sympathetic or paternalistic local authority employers, were very successful in resisting moves towards grant-maintained schools, and in many cases governing bodies in local authority-maintained schools chose to 'opt in' to local arrangements that meant individual schools simply adopted policies negotiated with unions at local authority level. Meanwhile, local union officers were generally able to continue to access 'facilities time' (the system of release time for union officers to undertake union duties) and the historically high levels of union density among teachers were holding up. Given these developments, the NUT was under little pressure to change as, on the surface at least, 'business as usual' appeared to not only prevail, but be sustainable. This in part explains the NUT's initial ambivalence towards the shift to organising models in the wider trade union movement, exemplified by the establishment of the TUC's Organising Academy. For many unions, devastated by deindustrialisation or privatisation, the need for new approaches was an obvious imperative. The NUT appeared to be under no equivalent pressure.

THE NUT'S 'TURN TO ORGANISING': BUILDING WORKPLACE POWER

Driven by relative falling membership share in comparison to the NASUWT, an ageing local officer base and the union's struggle to assert influence from its position outside of the Social Partnership, the process of making the 'turn to organising' unfolded through a series of conference decisions and internal reviews from 2004 onwards. Early iterations of what it meant to be an 'organising union' were often ambiguous as the union wrestled with clarifying the purpose: was the focus membership gain, renewing local structures or building workplace capacity? The imperative for the NUT to face up to the need for a transformative organising model, however, came in 2010 with the election of the Coalition government and the radical change in the school system this brought with it. Deep cuts to local authorities' budgets introduced austerity measures at the centre of the school system, while the new government's drive to make all schools academies threatened to change beyond recognition the local authority-based industrial relations system that still prevailed despite all the changes since 1988. Many local union officers, who had access to established negotiating machinery, often with facilities time to undertake union duties, found their circumstances changed almost overnight. Of course, there was considerable variability across the country, but in many instances, the impact on union capacity and organisation was dramatic. This situation is reflected graphically in the response of one local division secretary, who described being in a local authority that had axed all facilities time and aggressively encouraged its own schools to become academies:

> I have gone from being a union officer with full-time facilities and dealing with one employer [the local authority] to having no facilities time at all and having to deal with 200 employers [newly academised schools].[3]

Prior to these reforms, NUT divisions were organised to represent union members in negotiations with their employers. These bodies were typically coterminous with the employing local authority, and by definition, each division dealt with a single employer. By 2014, this situation had already changed dramatically. For example, in the Midlands and South West regions, each local division was dealing with an average of 28 different employers. In the Eastern region, the equivalent figure was 37 employers. The impact on union organisation and resources was immediate and dramatic.

The challenges for the union were being posed very starkly. The attacks on teachers' working conditions, pay and pensions were substantial and demanded serious member mobilisation, but the environment for union organising was becoming increasingly fragmented, with local activists being forced to fight on multiple fronts (both in terms of the range of issues, and the number of employers). The union had taken national strike action over pay on 24 April 2008, the first national strike since the suspension of national collective bargaining rights, and the union also played a leading role in the 2011 pensions strikes, including the public sector-wide strike on 30 November 2011, when 60% of England's schools were closed completely. However, despite the visibility of these national actions, it was becoming increasingly apparent that in the new fragmented school system, national action had to be built on much stronger workplace organisation.

Some of the impulse for this new workplace organising emerged from the state's drive to academise schools and the local campaigns of resistance that developed as a response. For some time there had been a tradition of mobilising highly effective local union–community coalitions against schools 'opting out' to become grant-maintained, and this was replicated when academies emerged as the successor to grant-maintained schools. The academies issue was more challenging, not least because the state had removed the requirement for a parental ballot and also taken on the power to 'force' some schools to academise (for a discussion of the factors impacting the success, or otherwise, of anti-academies campaigns, see Muna, 2017). However, there were still a significant number of local campaigns that emerged when plans to academise particular schools were announced. Perhaps the most high-profile of these was the campaign at Downhills School in North London in 2012, when union members in the school worked with local parents to form a powerful union–community coalition to challenge the forced academisation of their school. The combination of a well-organised staff (the school had 100% NUT membership and there were good relations between teachers and support staff, organised in Unison) working with a parents' group that was galvanised by the attack on their school ('We were so angry – we were furious' – Downhills parent[4]) provided the basis of a local campaign that attracted national interest. As with many community-based anti-academies actions, the key figures in the campaign were overwhelmingly women, who often emerged as 'reluctant leaders' (Stevenson, 2016) in the face of threats to the ethos of their community school.

The Downhills campaign was ultimately unsuccessful (having taken its case as far as the High Court), and in many ways it illustrated the difficulties of localised campaigns having to confront a state apparatus that had given itself huge legal powers. However, the experience provided inspiration for many other campaigns against academisation (several of which were successful) and also contributed to shifting the dynamic in the academies debate (with the government subsequently retreating from its commitment to academise all schools following a broad-based political campaign and national action from the NUT). Another example, of several, was provided by a school in the East Midlands where staff challenged the efforts of their governors to opt to become an academy by taking eight days of strike action. Again the campaign was not success-ful, but the NUT rep at the time of the dispute (and who only took on the rep's role during the campaign) was adamant that the dispute had made the union group stronger. Membership increased from 15 to 35 members during the period of the strikes, and after the dispute, management knew they could no longer take the staff for granted:

> although the school became an academy we were able to hold the gov-ernors to so many things … we maintained that pressure on them … so the school hasn't really changed a lot after academisation. The gov-ernors have adopted the joint union pay policy, they have brought back in the facilities time budget and we have got lots of new activists in the school who are members of the division now.[5]

After the event, the school rep identified the unfavourable context for organising in the school at the start of the campaign (the relatively small NUT group, for example), but argued that the situation was transformed by active union organising. Her conclusions, based on her reflections of that experience are highlighted at the opening of this chapter – 'If you can organise my school – you can organise anywhere.'

Another very visible example of how the NUT was beginning to connect union action with union-building emerged in 2012 when Not-tingham City Council published plans to impose a five-term year across all its schools (replacing the original model based on three terms). NUT members in the city immediately began to organise to resist this development in a campaign that simultaneously focused on developing workplace organisation among members and building coalitions with parents' groups, including Parents Against the 5 Term Year. The campaign itself combined high-profile parent-led actions with strike action by NUT members across Nottingham schools. The union branch had built assid-uously for industrial action, and by the time strike action was organised, the union had strengthened its collective capacity considerably. Between March and November 2012, the union increased membership by 14% in schools involved in the strikes and the proportion of schools with an NUT rep had increased dramatically from 31% to 72%. Sheena Wheatley, secretary of Nottingham City NUT, and colleagues, commented:

For us in Nottingham City NUT, the lessons are clear: collective disputes with a clear plan of action, imaginative organising and a 'capacity building' focus are essential if we are to defend the interests of teachers, students and the wider school communities.[6]

The need to develop a national industrial action strategy combined with a commitment to workplace organising began to develop further during 2013–2014 when the NUT worked alongside the NASUWT (one of the three main teacher unions) to oppose government proposals on pay and working conditions. The campaign involved strike action in autumn 2013 (with the NASUWT) and in July 2014 (NUT only), but it also involved the use of 'action short of strike' (ASOS), whereby members were expected to work to rule to push back against unreasonable workloads.

The union's 2013–2014 industrial action campaign relied heavily on the actions of school reps. Only reps possessed the local knowledge of the issues in their particular school, and therefore could organise their own members collectively in order to challenge excessive workload. This was, however, risky as in 2009 only 27% of schools in England had an identifiable school rep. By 2014, after much focused work by the union, that figure had risen to 42%, with reps in 72% of secondary schools and 32% of primary schools. Moreover 2,000 new reps had been trained using a substantially revised training programme that focused on actively collectivising at the workplace (and was located in a more explicitly political critique of neoliberal education reforms). At the time, the union's approach to organising was captured in a series of articles by General Secretary Christine Blower in the *Morning Star* in April 2014. The articles emphasised the commitment to lay-led activism, a deepening of union democracy and the development of issues-based organising at the workplace. Setting out the NUT's approach to organising, Christine Blower asserted:

organising is defined as the identification, development and empowerment of local lay leaders, who, through the collective mobilisation of members around issues of concern to them, both improve the working lives of members and rebuild lay union structures on a participative basis.

Implicit within the organising model is recognition of the fundamentally antagonistic relationship between employer and employee.[7]

The significance of the second paragraph above should not be underestimated. It explicitly rejected the years of *rapprochement* and positioned the NUT as an activist union committed to building union power to challenge the power of employers and the state.

The union's industrial action campaign in 2013–2014 was, perhaps inevitably, uneven, reflecting the very variable level of union organisation across schools as the process of rebuilding progressed. However, what was clear was that the campaign provided excellent opportunities to build workplace organisation, and this was most likely when local branch officers worked strategically with their school reps to build collective capacity at the workplace. One such initiative was developed in Coventry, where the union worked across both local authority and academy schools to develop a 'workload charter'. The initiative responded to a very real problem for members relating to workload, but Coventry union officers were clear that the project was ultimately about union-building at the workplace. Participation in the project required schools to commit to establish a 'workload committee' (described by one local union officer as a school based joint negotiating committee 'by any other name') to monitor and address workload concerns, and each group required union representation, which immediately embedded workplace representation in the system:

I think that we have always been quite clear that this initiative is just another tool, and the thing that is going to win for our members is getting that organisation into schools. This is a tool – not the silver bullet. If we get the schools organised – then we can make a difference in those schools.[8]

The same officer went on to argue that such a way of working involved a different type of relationship between local officers and school reps, whereby local officers made space to work with reps so that reps felt able to organise members collectively in their workplace. This contrasted with historic models, in which reps had often been encouraged to pass problems at the workplace up to branch officers. Now the emphasis was on building collective power in the workplace in a way that gave members the confidence to collectivise at school level, and to see themselves as the solution to the problems they faced. A key role of local officers was to build that workplace confidence, rather than encourage a 'leave it to "the union'" dependency culture among members. As one Coventry officer commented:

> I think what we found out is that we did a hell of a lot of work in the run up to the last [industrial action] ballot, and I think that what we realised was at that point we tend to fall into two different modes … like a war footing and a peace footing. I think that what we have realised is that we have got to have that kind of 'ever ready' footing all the time and be constantly putting those dates in the diary and getting into schools to talk to our reps. I know it is easier said than done, but we need to make sure that we are doing that … because where we do get into those schools, and recruit the reps, it does make a difference.

In the new fragmented schools landscape, building workplace power became an obvious necessity, and it was equally clear that there could be no building such power without developing the role of the school rep. Here we offer an example of how one teacher, Kate, was drawn into union activity, and how her actions as a union rep helped members in her workplace to push back against encroaching managerialism and to redefine the frontier of control at her school.[9]

Kate's Story

Kate had been teaching for 17 years, and in her school for 12 years. For the last seven years she had been the school NUT representative, during which time the size of NUT membership had grown considerably. Kate took on the role of rep when the school announced redundancies and invited reps to statutory consultation meetings. The NUT had no rep at the time, and in the absence of anyone else willing to take it on, Kate agreed to represent the union at the meeting and subsequently to become the rep. At that point, the key support was provided by her local association secretary – 'without her I would not have had the confidence'. Her experience highlights the critical role that local officers can play in developing the capacity of workplace reps.

Initially, Kate indicated that relations with the headteacher were cordial, although from the outset the headteacher had made clear his anti-union attitudes ('he told me unions were anathema to him'). However, as the linked pressures of inspection and budget cuts combined, staff at the school found themselves under more pressure, with greater scrutiny of their work. Kate began to organise members to challenge particular issues collectively as they developed, explicitly using the threat of industrial action to strengthen bargaining power. The union group had used an indicative ballot for strike action to oppose redundancies, and Kate organised similar mobilisations to challenge new plans for covering the classes of absent staff, the use of a 'mocksted' (a 'dummy run' Ofsted inspection using private sector consultants), proposals for classroom observations, a change to the staff dress code and the use of student test scores as appraisal targets.

A key lesson from Kate's story was her experience of mobilising members across a broad range of issues, many of them combining both the 'industrial' and 'professional' dimensions of teachers' work. For Kate, the key issue was about teachers' control of their own work, and what she described as a process of 'deprofessionalisation', driven by increased managerialism. Challenging these multiple initiatives was as much about protecting professional autonomy as it was about resisting rising workloads. For Kate, the two issues were inseparable. Describing the union group's refusal to co-operate with classroom observations, Kate commented that once armed with the ballot result, '[we] said that we were going to refuse to let them into the classroom'. In an untypically clear example, the frontier of control had literally been drawn at the classroom door.

Kate was able to continue to build up membership in her school and to mobilise members around key issues. She did not pretend it was easy, but argued that her members understood the need to maintain a united collective front, and so could be relied on when tested. As the union group scored its victories, persuading colleagues that union membership and collective action made a difference became an easier argument to win. The evidence was there. She continues to be guided by the lessons she learned from her early experience:

Reps in schools – organising, supporting, recruiting, training, building them up – so they know what they fight on, what they can win on. Have a win. Right, next. Build yourselves up. That has to be where we focus our energies.

Sharing stories such as Kate's so that activists could learn from, and gain confidence from, the experiences of others became an important element of grassroots organising and building in the union. One important example of this type of activity was a fringe event held at the 2016 Annual Conference called 'Winning in Schools', sponsored by more than 50 local associations. The event showcased the experiences of a range of school reps who had successfully used the ASOS guidelines in place at the time to organise collectively at their workplace around workload issues. It was also highly popular, with its inclusive approach welcomed by those who understood the need for open discussion about navigating new challenges. The fringe event was then followed up by a one-day national conference in Manchester with the same title, and again sponsored by a large number of local associations. The conference was attended by 150 workplace reps, many of whom shared their own experiences of organising in the new schools environment, and their successful campaigns on ASOS.

The 'Winning in Schools' events exemplified the demand from local association activists for the union to prioritise building workplace capacity, and this in turn was reflected in a series of motions at annual conferences that called for union support to develop workplace organising. In 2017, 2018 and 2019, motions recognising the central role of workplace organisation and the school rep, and the need to support rep recruitment and development, topped the prioritisation poll in the Membership and Organising section of the NUT's conference agenda, demonstrating that the commitment to the organising agenda was increasingly being driven by the union's activist base. Among demands made in these motions, the 2019 motion called for the development of a 'Workplace Representation Strategy'[10] focused on supporting local officers to build a visible and effective presence in every workplace through recruitment and support for schools reps.

WORKPLACE REPS MAKING A DIFFERENCE: THE VIRTUOUS CIRCLE OF WORKPLACE ORGANISATION

Kate's story provides a very tangible example of what the new workplace organising could look like, and the central role of the school rep in building this culture in the union. Nor was her experience isolated, with a growing number of examples of effective workplace organising. However, the case for this approach needed to be based on more than just anecdote, and this evidential base emerged in 2017 from a research project assessing the NUT's organising strategy.[11] The research sought to better understand how member commitment and participation could be developed as the basis for developing union power. One aspect of the research was a survey of 355 union members and 458 union representatives across seven local associations to develop a measure or 'scale' of member commitment and participation ('commitment' reflected identification with the union, and 'participation' addressed issues of involvement and activity).[12] The scale is presented in Figure 4.1. At the top of the figure is the statement that members were least likely to respond to positively ('I regularly attend local association meetings'). At the foot of the figure is the statement that members were most likely to respond to positively ('the union exists for teachers like me'). Depending on an individual's survey responses, it was possible to allocate each member to a point on the scale. At this point, the member was very likely to agree with the survey statements below that point, but very unlikely to agree with any statements above that point. Those placed closer to the top of the scale had a higher commitment and participation 'score', while those placed nearer the bottom had a lower one.

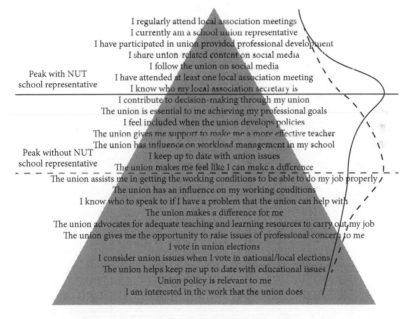

Figure 4.1   Member commitment and participation scale

The real utility of this data depended on whether it was possible to identify what variables might correlate with commitment and participation. In short, was it possible to identify what factors could help us understand why a member was allocated to a higher, or lower, point on the scale, and therefore was more, or less, likely to be involved in the union?

What emerged from the data analysis was that *only one factor* showed a statistically significant relationship with levels of membership commitment and participation – and that was the presence of a workplace representative. No other factor (demographic factors such as age and sex, school type etc.) showed this relationship. It is illustrated in Figure 4.1 by the two lines that go from the base to the top of the diagram (one solid and one hatched). These lines show the distribution of responses when presented in the form of vertically arranged distribution curves.[13] The graphic illustrates that in those schools with an NUT rep (solid line, skewed towards the top), union members were more likely to show higher levels of commitment and participation. Where there was no union rep (hatched line, skewed towards the bottom), the distribution pointed to lower levels of commitment and participation. No other factor showed this relationship.

This relationship is not presented in terms of a simple 'cause and effect'. What it suggests, however, is an iterative relationship that runs both ways (hence, creating a virtuous circle). Where there is a workplace rep, this supports member commitment and participation, which in turn is more likely to ensure the school always has a rep (when, for example, a rep stands down or leaves the school). By contrast, the absence of a rep is likely to lead to a long-term decline in member commitment and participation, making it more difficult to recruit a rep. The result is a vicious cycle of decline that can be difficult to arrest and reverse.

Another key finding from the research demonstrated that the closer union activists were to the workplace, the more likely they were to reflect the diversity of the workforce. For example, the research showed that across the seven local associations, 61% of school reps were women, which was below the overall proportion of the workforce, but was higher than corresponding figures for activism elsewhere in the union. Moreover, on other indicators, such as age, ethnicity and sexual orientation, NUT school reps were more likely to be younger, Black or LGBT+ than the membership as a whole. This is important for multiple reasons, but in particular because it is difficult to see how the NUT can build solidarity if members do not see the union as an organisation that they can relate to and identify with. Contrast this with the experience of one young union member in the same study who described going to a local branch meeting and reflecting, having looked at those at the 'top table', that 'the union didn't look like me'. This research suggests that alongside all the steps being taken by trade unions to ensure they represent the diversity of their membership at all levels, one of the most effective strategies to these ends is the recruitment and development of workplace reps. This is important as an end in itself, but also because these roles can act as a pipeline into wider activist roles in the union.

In many senses, the 2017 research provides no more than an evidential base for what many union activists have always instinctively understood. However, the logic of the analysis arguably posed the issues much more starkly than had previously been the case. The clear implication was that workplace reps are both an indicator and a source of union power at the workplace. They not only make a difference, but in a hyper-fragmented school system, they may make *the* difference in terms of delivering collective action. Furthermore, it is important to recognise that in the survey discussed above, a simple distinction is made between having a school rep and having no rep. In reality, some reps will be much more active/ effective than others, but the survey did not allow for this qualitative differentiation. Here we speculate, hopefully uncontroversially, that where reps feel confident to take on a more active role, then the 'rep effect' will be correspondingly greater. Put simply, if reps make a difference, then more confident and active reps will make *more* difference. In presenting this argument, we highlight the importance of rep support and development (rep recruitment is only a part of the process), and in the NEU/ NUT's case, we would identify the union's revised reps training programme as making a particular contribution. The programme had been significantly revised in 2014 and focused much more on the role of reps as leaders in their school, accompanied by a sharper and explicit political analysis of the issues driving the policy agenda in schools. No longer was the course framed as a 'Rep's Survival Guide' (as the original course materials were titled), but rather reps were encouraged to collectivise members' grievances and directly challenge the frontier of control at the workplace. As one rep commented:

> The course was invaluable ... brilliant. After the Advanced course I went back into my school and I said to myself 'Right – nobody is going to put me down after this one.' I felt I knew so much.[14]

We have limited space here to discuss the revision of the reps' training programme in detail, but readers can find a comprehensive discussion of the issues in Little and McDowell (2017).

THE 'REP EFFECT' IN ACTION

This 'rep effect' manifests itself in schools with reps in myriad ways every day, although sometimes in ways that are small and imperceptible. For example, management often choose *not* to do something for fear of union resistance, but this consequence of union power is largely invisible. However, on a larger scale, the benefits of rep organisation were illustrated very visibly in January 2020 when NEU members in Tower Hamlets were balloted for industrial action over proposed cuts to redundancy terms. The issue was not an easy one to organise around, but it represented a direct attack on terms and conditions, and therefore needed to be resisted. The union's initial campaign was based on an indicative ballot intended to establish whether there was sufficient member support for action in the event of a full ballot. Of course, such ballots also send their own signals to employers about the strength of member commitment to the union.

In total, there were 1,249 NEU members distributed across 63 different schools and workplaces (including in local authority central services). These figures highlight many of the issues faced when organising in the school sector, with membership spread over a large number of workplaces. Although London borough branches are more geographically concentrated than many other branches, issues of geography remain significant. The challenges for local officers to get into large numbers of schools in a relatively short time period were substantial. Hence, the Tower Hamlets campaign was driven through the branch's school reps, with named reps in 52 of the 63 workplaces (covering 89% of the ballot group).

Throughout the balloting period, branch officers co-ordinated the 'Get The Vote Out' (GTVO) campaign and managed the key campaign communications, but school reps were the ones who were able to have direct face-to-face contact with members in their workplaces and who played the key role in mobilising the vote. The campaign was successful, with a 54% ballot return and an emphatic 97% vote in favour of strike action, which resulted in the issue being resolved without taking action. However, what was particularly significant was the relationship between voter turnout and school rep activity. As part of its GTVO campaign, the branch sought to track voting patterns as accurately as possible, and when this data was linked to rep activity, the pattern was clear. For the purpose of the analysis, the branch distinguished between three types of rep: those who were highly engaged, including attending branch meetings, those who had more limited branch contact, and those who had virtually no branch contact. When voting figures were cross-tabulated against this categorisation of reps, it was clear that high voting figures (returns of 75%+) came from schools with engaged reps, while poor turnouts were overwhelmingly associated with schools where there was no named rep, or a rep with little evidence of branch engagement.[15]

Branch Secretary Alex Kenny was clear that the successful ballot result depended on reps getting the vote out, and that without this level of organisation, the ballot threshold would not have been met and the dispute would not have been resolved successfully. He commented:

We knew we were taking a chance with the ballot, but we were confident that we could get close to the ballot thresholds because of the relationship we have built with reps over a number of years. We have developed a high degree of trust amongst our active reps and we don't take them for granted. With more and more decisions being taken at school level we took a strategic decision in our district to turn to schools and deepen our workplace organising and the ballot result was one of the fruits of that work.[16]

BUILDING POWER IN A HYPER-FRAGMENTED SCHOOL SYSTEM: ORGANISING IN 'ACADEMY LAND'

In January 2021, the scale of the changes in the schools landscape were to some extent clear – neoliberal restructuring had atomised the system while removing democratic control from local authorities. However, although 37% of primary schools were academy schools, with the equivalent proportion for secondary schools at 78%, the situation was also becoming more complex as academy schools were increasingly forming into groups of schools called Multi-Academy Trusts (MATs).[17] We have tried to describe how such developments have posed obvious threats, but also opportunities. Recognising McCarthy's (1966, p. 62) classic statement that 'In general terms it can be said that trade unions seek to bargain at the level at which effective decisions are made', the growth in academisation has provided an opportunity to connect organising as a strategy with changes in organisational form that placed union democracy at the heart of the project. In summary, the shift in the frontier of control has opened up opportunities to connect members in workplaces with the union, and to increase democratic engagement in the process. The commitment to open up this opportunity was reflected most obviously in an internal paper adopted by the NUT's National Executive in which it set out its commitment to building new structures to deal with the impact of mass academisation and the growth of MATs, and which opened up opportunities to deepen union democracy:

Democracy, participation and representation: ensuring any new academy chain structure is lay led and accountable to the membership

The question of union democracy has a fundamental relationship to the vision and shape of the sort of union the NUT wants to be in a rapidly changing education landscape. A union that posits itself as an organising, campaigning, lay led organisation needs to work to ensure that any new structures necessitated by changes in the industrial relations landscape we operate in, maintain and promote the idea that union democracy is based upon a continuous process rooted in the lived daily experiences of teachers, and that decisions taken by the Union which impact upon members are democratically arrived at and implemented by members.

In terms of structures within academy chains, a model based upon participatory democracy would best guarantee the Union's stated strategic objectives of being a campaigning lay led union.[18]

This position statement from the National Executive was significant because it made a specific, and radical, commitment to developing new forms of workplace-based democracy with union policy 'democratically arrived at and implemented by members'. The paper passed by the Executive quoted directly from Peter Fairbrother's classic work on union democracy *All Those in Favour* (1984) referred to in Chapter 2 and represented a genuine attempt to connect system reform, organisational change and union renewal through the development of participatory democracy.

Alongside the changes in organisational form, the union also looked to network school reps working in academies more horizontally, in particular so that reps working in Multi-Academy Trusts could organise alongside other reps facing the same employer. A significant moment in this process was when the union organised its first event solely for the reps that were working in the leading MATs. This day-long event, called *Chainlinks*, provided a political understanding of why fragmentation and liberalisation was happening as well as helping to develop strategic responses to academisation and the growth of MATs. The day showed that there was still a tension between established organisational structures and the new structures the union was hoping to build. For example, reps in the same chain, despite working for the same employer, typically did not know each other. This was often because they belonged to a different NUT division.

It was clear that many of the reps who attended the event gained a clear insight into how to build collectively in the new fragmented industrial relations environment. A rep's evaluation from the *Chainlinks* event encapsulated this:

Was this the day that the union was given back to the membership? Well, it felt like that to me.

It's clear that the traditional ways of bargaining at a national and local authority level are changing. What replaces it is on the one hand quite ominous, but also quite empowering.

Increasingly in the future it will be down to union members to organise themselves and take up the cause at school and academy-chain level, as well as within local authorities.

As a consequence, the union has to adapt and this is all about engaging reps and members on the issues that are most pressing.

The days of waiting for 'the union' to do it for us are disappearing fast. I left the day having made some firm connections with colleagues and feeling that what I always wanted to be true had been reaffirmed — the union belongs to the members and it's the members who will determine what happens next.

In practice, the possibilities for renewal that opened up as the school system fragmented have often been difficult to realise, and the systemic divisions and tensions that have been intentionally created as a means to weaken education union organisation have been difficult to overcome. Here we identify four issues that have emerged from these experiences and that point to the need for deeper and more effective workplace organising activity, but also the need to build unity across the whole system, both at MAT level and nationally.

1. A Hostile Environment

The new schools landscape has created a hostile environment for trade union organisation in which industrial relations systems have been dismantled, schools compete against each other for survival, and managerial authority has been strengthened. Cultures of collegiality have been replaced by cultures of expected compliance. Those who challenge this are too often exposed to bullying and intimidation, with all the consequences of this for trade union organisation. This bullying and discrimination are often gendered and racialised. We have argued previously that the fragmentation of the school system was driven by a class-based strategy to defeat organised teachers. This has not been successful, but there can be no question that school-based organising is only a building block, and on its own it cannot overcome the consequences of system-wide fragmentation.

2. The Contradictions and Limitations of School-based Decision-making

While the 2010 reforms enshrined a fragmented education system and greater 'freedoms' for individual school managers around terms and conditions, these freedoms were limited by the system as a whole. That is, on central issues of school funding and teacher pay, these are still, at the level of a 'cost envelope', decided at national level by government. Likewise, schools cannot opt out of the high-stakes assessment and accountability regime. Courageous management and/or strong union activity can mitigate against the worst practices, but the pressure remains within the system. So while the frontier of control has been devolved increasingly to school level, it is a type of decision-making that remains fundamentally constrained by the central state. This clearly poses significant challenges if strategy focuses exclusively on building at the workplace.

3. A Contested Agenda

The changes we have described represented a significant change in direction for the union, and it would be naïve to assume these changes had universal support. Some diligent local officers who had carried out casework for literally countless members did not believe the membership could be mobilised in the ways that we are describing. This analysis sought to secure the best deals possible through broadly constructive engagement with employers while maintaining membership through the provision of casework. Such an approach was not sustainable, however, as arrangements with employers often started from a point of weakness (a passive membership and declining activist base) while the exponential growth of casework ensured officers could not keep up with demand for support. Other sections of the union were sceptical about a significant increase in paid organisers at the same time when lay officers were experiencing cuts in facilities time. Did this not represent a shift in power away from a lay activist base and towards the union's bureaucracy? Others again were sceptical about both the willingness and ability of school-based reps to take on a more expansive role, especially across Multi Academy Trusts, where, despite the theoretical aspiration to build MAT-based democratic and negotiating structures, the preservation of schools within a MAT contributing to established facilities time arrangements was often prioritised in practice. These tensions continue, and highlight the limitations of transformative change being delivered from the centre. In our opinion, it is a danger which can only be countered by developing real grassroots leadership of the organising project – an issue we will return to in later chapters.

4. The Focus on Consequences, Not Causes

A final problem faced by the focus on workplace organisation, and perhaps the most fundamental, was that it sought to respond to the consequences of the neoliberal restructuring of schools without addressing the causes: the ideology of neoliberalism itself. Any efforts by workers to contest the frontier of control will always represent a challenge to neoliberal logic, but the danger is that such conflicts represent no more than a skirmish within a wider set of parameters that remain largely uncontested. Every challenge opens up the possibility of connecting immediate struggles with wider questions about the prevailing system, but often such struggles remain isolated industrially and ideologically – industrially because within the English school system, trade union struggles cannot be easily connected at a local, let alone national, level, and ideologically because industrial struggles cannot be relied on to develop spontaneously into a more profound critique of the system. Two consequences flow from the analysis. First, there is a need to think through how workplace organising can be 'scaled up' on a level that has been difficult to achieve since the chronic fragmentation of the system. Second, there is a need to explicitly confront the corrosive nature of neoliberal ideology in the public education system. This battle of ideas needs to be waged within the system among the workforce (where dominant ideas are often reluctantly accepted and become normalised), but it must also look outwards, to parents and the wider community.

WORKPLACE ORGANISATION: NECESSARY …
BUT NOT SUFFICIENT

The NUT, and more recently the NEU, have responded strategically to several decades of neoliberal restructuring of English state education: reforms that were in large part motivated by a drive to weaken, marginalise and even eradicate trade union organisation and influence. The NUT was arguably slow to respond to these developments as it sought to hold on to a system it had fought hard to secure and was reluctant to adapt to a future it was, quite rightly and understandably, trying to resist. However, in refusing to recognise the need to reconfigure and renew, specifically in relation to the development of workplace organisation, the union lost vital time. Although the union seemed able to retain traditional structures for negotiating at local authority level, the reality was that these structures were already losing influence and the union's activist base was both shrinking and ageing. From the outside it may have appeared as though the union was in good shape, but beneath the surface its organisational base was in decline.

By 2010, and the onset of both austerity and academisation, the NUT had no alternative but to consider how it must rebuild organisational power, hence the union's 'turn to organising' and its efforts to reconnect with members and seriously build workplace power. This has been a long, slow and uneven process. To borrow a phrase from Jane McAlevey, it is manifestly clear there are 'no shortcuts'. However, the union has seen an influx of new, often younger, activists as it has sought to develop workplace organisation while also creating a more inclusive culture by creating organising forums for young educators, LGBT+, disabled and Black workers. The union's strategic direction meant that it was well placed in particular to organise to support members when the COVID-19 pandemic struck in 2020 (discussed in Chapter 6). This allowed the union to significantly increase membership and workplace representative density, which provided the basis for some significant successes during the period when the pandemic was at its height.

Workplace organisation based on active union organisation in which members engage and act collectively to challenge the frontier of control that curtails their professional autonomy and drives up their workload is clearly the bedrock of collective action. Where such cultures do not exist, it is difficult to see how collective resistance, in any form and at any level, can develop. Hence our claim that strong workplace organisation, built around workplace representatives who feel confident to act as local leaders in their workplace, has been essential to NEU/NUT's renewal. There can be no understanding of how the union has built union power, and how it must continue to build further, without recognising the central role of workplace organisation. It is literally the foundation on which all else is built.

At the same time, we must also recognise that this alone is not enough because workplace organising must ultimately provide the base for building solidarity across the system while connecting workplace concerns with a political critique of neoliberalism and demands for an education system based on equality and democracy. Hence, while focusing on workplace organising as the foundational basis of solidarity and collective action, we must also look *beyond organising* in order to develop a trade unionism that is capable of mounting a more fundamental challenge to the current system with all the inequalities of class, race and sex that are hardwired into existing social relations.

5

Breaking Neoliberal Hegemony in Education

two particular individuals have influenced me more than any others.

The Italian Marxist thinker – and father of Euro-Communism – Antonio Gramsci.

And the reality television star Jade Goody.

The above are the words of Michael Gove in an address to the Social Market Foundation, a right-wing think tank, in February 2013 (significantly titled 'The Progressive Betrayal'[1]). At the time, Gove was the Conservative Secretary of State for Education, and his speech was intended to surprise and provoke. Jade Goody had become a household name as a controversial reality TV star who had died aged 27 of cervical cancer. Gove asserted that Goody had been failed by the education system and that, recognising the negative impact poor schooling had on her life, Goody had used the money from her short TV career to make sure that her children would receive a 'better' education by sending them to private school. Gove mourned the fact that such schools were beyond the reach of the majority, and wanted to 'improve' the state sector to give all children – at risk of being failed by 'the Blob'[2] of the educational establishment – access to a 'great' education. This, as we know, was to be achieved by breaking up the local authority school system and replacing these schools with academies. The creation of competition within the system would then, following neoliberal dogma, lead to the panacea of 'constant improvement'.

But whereas Gove used Jade Goody to justify structural change in education delivery, he used Antonio Gramsci to justify his equally radical pedagogical reforms. We have used Gramsci's ideas as a political thinker and activist, but his work frequently engaged with educational issues – indeed, this dimension of Gramsci's writing cannot be separated from his political ideas and activity. Gramsci's views on education are complex and controversial, and have been used by some on the political right to justify a focus on educational 'basics' (reading, writing and maths) and a 'knowledge'-based curriculum.[3] Of course Michael Gove's appropriation of Gramsci made no effort to place Gramsci's ideas in their historical context, nor to acknowledge Gramsci's view that understanding and critiquing the knowledge of dominant groups was a preliminary step in a larger process of revolutionary change (for this discussion, see Stevenson, 2023). Rather, the minister was only interested in securing headlines and baiting political opponents, and on both counts he could probably be judged successful.

However, ironically, the NUT was also engaging with the ideas of Antonio Gramsci during this period, although in a way that *was* concerned with securing long-term radical change, not short-term political capital. Elements within the NUT, both elected national and local officers and staff, adopted a very different interpretation of the thinking of Gramsci: using his concept of hegemony (see Chapter 3), and reflecting on how it is constructed, and can be contested. The aim was to think more deeply about how to deal with the underlying causes of the neoliberal education reforms that were creating so many problems for the union and its members. This theorisation of the NUT's organising work was a conscious effort to break from the pull of 'pragmatic' answers to the difficult and complex situation the union found itself in. Under the assault of Gove, the union would often find itself pinned down by both an intensified routinisation of having to respond to the day-to-day issues of trade union representation that resulted from increasing 'managerialism' in schools (the pull to *rapprochement*), and, because of the speed of the change happening and a legacy of practice, the over-reliance upon traditional methods to counter Gove's attacks (the pull to resistance). If the union were to develop a renewal strategy that attempted to deal with both causes and consequences simultaneously, building the confidence and self-activity of the widest possible layer of members, a theoretical touchstone was needed, to help it see beyond the pressures of the 'now' and to help chart a course to affect longer-term change.

The starting point for this process of critical analysis was threefold. First, there was an acceptance of the scale of the task. The union was setting itself the goal of system change within education, which meant getting government, and indeed opposition parties as potential parties of government, to change policies they had been wedded to for decades. Second, a re-evaluation of how neoliberal education had become so dominant was needed to understand how the union could go about shifting the political discourse around education. And third, the question of the consciousness of teachers and their willingness, or otherwise, to be part of moves to deliver system change was essential to a union that put a premium on the self-activity of members as the agents of change. The conceptual tools associated with Gramsci's work helped sections of the union's leadership work through these issues. We are not claiming here that the process of renewal we discuss in this book was guided by some tidy Gramscian plan, but we are arguing that the ideas of Gramsci were being engaged with and provided useful and influential frameworks for activists and officers to consider how to both understand the immediate situation and to build a movement capable of creating something better.

One very practical example of this mix of theory and practice was the development of a training course for NUT local officers entitled *What Can We Really Learn from Antonio Gramsci?*, first rolled out at the annual briefing of local association/division secretaries in the autumn of 2013. The training was a direct riposte to Michael Gove's hijacking of Gramsci to support his reactionary objectives. During the course, participants took part in a 'card sort' exercise where they were asked to place model answers to a number of headings in two columns: one column for what they thought the government's position was, and the other column for what the NUT's position was (see Table 5.1).

In Table 5.1, the sections of text in the first column were taken directly from various DfE publications or ministerial speeches, and those in the second column were taken from NUT publications. A number of points became apparent to those participating in the training. First, it made clear the ideological basis of human capital theory that was shaping education (and many immediately recognised that this was a narrative that dominated society more broadly); second, participants recognised that in its own terms, the neoliberal narrative was largely coherent, and thus potentially convincing; third, while participants recognised the neoliberal narrative as shaping their lived experience, the majority disagreed with it, both in principle and in consequence. Following the training, participants could more readily compare the world as it was with the world as union members wanted it to be, and so begin to more effectively analyse what would be necessary to 'break' the dominant model.

Table 5.1   Statements provided for NUT training 'card sort' exercise (in sorted format)

	Government statements	NUT statements
Standard testing	Is a necessary pre-condition of informing consumer choice based upon quantitative measures. It closes the gap within which failure and poor performance can be hidden from consumers.	Narrows the curriculum and focuses both teachers and pupils towards teaching and learning to the test. Assessment should support learning – learning should not be driven by assessment.
Performance-related pay	Is necessary to incentivise teachers and to reward good teaching practice. It will create a market environment where excellence will be rewarded.	Is divisive and will lead to a general lowering of morale. Teaching is a collaborative profession, and it is difficult to determine individual performance in isolation.
The purpose of school	To support pupils' investment in their human capital to best prepare them for a flexible and changing labour market, thus contributing to the economic success of themselves and the country.	To support pupils' growth towards ethically responsible membership of society, providing them with the knowledge and skills needed for life as well as work.
Competition between schools	Is necessary to drive up standards, identify failings and to give consumers a choice.	Creates a multi-levelled education service that tends to reinforce existing social divisions.
Parents	Will make a rational choice on which school to send their child to and should therefore be given as much information as possible about each school's performance.	Should feel assured that local schools will be well funded and work in a collaborative fashion with other schools and organisations. They should have the opportunity to participate in discussions and democratic decision-making processes.

In presenting this story, we are describing a process of transformation – not necessarily dramatic, perhaps quite modest, but definitely significant. It was a process in which participants stepped back from the 'noise' of their everyday life at school and began to deconstruct their experience of reality. In doing so, they were able to think critically about why the world they worked in did not align with the world they believed in and aspired to (what Gramsci referred to as 'contradictory consciousness'). In high-lighting this contradiction, and making it explicit, this simple card sort surfaced a frustration that could act as a spark to ignite further discussion and, crucially, action. But how to replicate this much more widely so that participants' experience on the training course of critiquing and reconstructing could be reproduced in some form on a much larger scale, within and beyond those who work in education?

BREAKING NEOLIBERAL HEGEMONY: BUILDING A 'COUNTER-HEGEMONIC' CAMPAIGN MODEL

The NUT's approach to campaigning sought nothing less than to break the consensus (to, literally, 'break the hegemony') that had dominated education policy since at least the mid-1980s, and to counterpose an education system that privileged the values of social justice and democracy and the value of education as a public good. This was inimical to a system that was based on competition and individualism, and on education as a commodity to be traded in a market. The challenge for the union was to build a movement that could begin to break the hegemony of neo-liberalism and the ideological structures sustaining it, and counterpose an alternative education system based on the values of social justice and democracy.

Our argument is that the strategy adopted by the NUT was Gramscian in inspiration and, in essence, was based upon an acceptance that the pre-dominant strategic option suited to the union's objective, and the context at that time, was that of a 'war of position' – that is, the union needed to contest neoliberal hegemony, and this engagement with neoliberal ideas could not be limited to the workplace, but needed to be taken into the political sphere (engaging with political parties), but also, and crucially, into communities. In summary, the union needed to make the case for what Gramsci (1971, p. 330) referred to as a 'higher conception of the world', with the union's campaigns being driven by its activists, organis-ing at the workplace around a political alternative. Furthermore, building civil society alliances around an alternative was critical to rebuilding union power.

The immediate context of the Gove reforms, and the response within the teaching profession and among some parents, inspired this approach and pointed to its potential in effecting change. Gove's plans provoked a battle of ideas within the profession, with teachers self-organising to challenge the curriculum and pedagogical reforms. Practitioner-driven research groups were springing up, and 'teach meets'[4] were being organised, all with the intention of networking like-minded teachers to challenge what was happening to their professional practice. There was a flourishing of social media accounts focused on what was happening within education, and 'edu-Twitter' became a real phenomenon, with some accounts garnering thousands of followers. Real-world events also took place, including *Northern Rocks*,[5] an annual weekend event that brought together hundreds of teachers to discuss what form 'good practice' could take within the constraints of the current system, but also what alternatives could look like beyond the current system. The weekend even witnessed a debate between Dominic Cummings, then Michael Gove's key adviser, and Kevin Courtney, the NUT's Deputy General Secretary at the time.

The union's approach, inspired by this context, was strategically formulated across three interdependent dimensions: terrains, levels and alliances (see Figure 5.1).

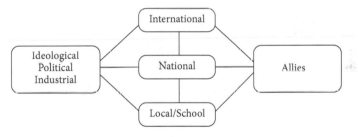

Figure 5.1   The NUT campaign model

First, it was recognised that the counter-hegemonic fight needed to take place across *three terrains*: the ideological, the political and the industrial/economic. At times, depending on context and an assessment of the balance of forces, the struggle might focus on one area, while at other times the struggle might be generalised across two or all three. The key point was that the three terrains were always interrelated and that the fight to secure hegemony would fail if the sole focus of the union's campaign activity was at the industrial or economic level, or if the political and ideological battle did not connect to the economic or industrial. It followed that the struggle would necessitate the NUT consciously trying to undermine the 'common sense' of neoliberal education policy and win popular support for its alternative vision of education. It could not just be *against*, it had to be *for* something too, and what it was for needed to connect with people's lived experiences, hopes and aspirations. The demands for an alternative must be rooted in exposing the injustices and inequalities of the prevailing *status quo*.

Second, the model presented in Figure 5.1 explained that the location of struggle was *multi-levelled*. England was both the pioneer country in implementing neoliberal education reforms and also the country where the reforms were most complete. However, across the globe, similar trends to those instigated in England in 1988 were clearly evident. The neoliberal reform movement, or GERM,[6] was a global phenomenon (Little, 2015). To build a counter-hegemonic model would necessitate a struggle locally, nationally and internationally, and where possible, practical solidarities needed to be built between and across the three levels. As a consequence, NUT training explicitly focused on the role of inter-governmental organisations, such as the World Bank and Organisation for Economic Co-operation and Development, as well as multinational 'edu-businesses', and demonstrated how these organisations acted globally to shape education policy in individual countries for ideological purposes and private gain. In practical terms, the union, alongside sister unions from Australia, Kenya, New Zealand, South Africa and the USA, played a central role in an international campaign to show the way in which the British education business Pearson influenced government policies in many countries while simultaneously selling 'policy solutions' to the same governments. NUT training intentionally also linked struggles across the global south and north, demonstrating how privatisation trends in the global north were being mirrored in the south, where international edu-businesses were aggressively promoting low-fee for-profit private schools in ways that directly undermined public education in some of the poorest parts of the world.

Third, the model affirmed that wherever possible, the NUT should work in principled alliances with others. This was to increase collective power while fighting on any particular issue, but also to engage in a dialogue around the union's wider vision of how education could be. Allies could be sister unions, parents' groups, or other civil society actors. The possibilities, limits and potential dangers of alliance-building were researched, and the principle established that while uniting with others around agreed aims, the union was clear it had its own independent view of the world – and strategies to change it – and that these would not be compromised for tactical gain.

Finally, underpinning the entire model was the understanding that the agents of change were to be local officers, workplace reps and members.

It should be stressed that this model was not constructed independently from, or separate to, the activity of grassroots members. Members were more often than not in advance of the union leadership in initiating and leading campaigns across all three terrains, sometimes achieving notable progress. What the national union was able to do was to generalise the lessons from these grassroots campaigns, both strengths and weaknesses, to help produce a coherent framework to help direct the work of the union as an organisation while also trying to help overcome the problems of scalability and generalisation identified by activists themselves.

Of course, models such as the one presented here remain abstract until they are tested in practice as a guide to action. This 'testing' became very visible in 2014 as the union tried to instrumentalise its counter-hegemonic model through its 'Stand Up For Education' campaign. At the heart of this campaign was an unambiguous appeal to a different education system than that currently on offer. An alternative was offered based upon values of equality and democracy. It was also clear that to go beyond dealing with the immediate consequences of neoliberal restructuring, the NUT needed to work with allies to build pressure on politicians while also retaining the right to take more direct strike action. The culmination of the campaign was to be an intervention in the 2015 general election. The strategy had been previously presented at the union's 2014 annual conference using the slogan 'Engage, pressure, strike',[7] and was elaborated in an internal NUT document later in the year:

> The NUT has a clear vision of what a high quality education service looks like. At its heart are the students we teach, a conception of teaching as a highly regarded profession, and a belief that society should be based around ideas of equality and fairness. These are not the values of the Global Education Reform Movement.
>
> The NUT's Stand Up For Education campaign is our strategic response to the domination of GERM. The campaign seeks to deal with both the immediate effects of education reform (workload; per-

formance related pay and so on) whilst organising to build a social movement to address the GERM systemically by offering a better vision of education than that currently being pursued by government.

Key to this strategy is reaching out to those who agree with us and those that can be won to our vision.[8]

The internal document went on to set out the NUT's approach to building a counter-hegemonic alliance. This crucially involved trying to unite the education workforce, and the document outlined the union's historic commitment to securing professional unity by working with other education unions. However, the union also made determined efforts to take its campaign to parents and the wider community, often through locally organised 'Question Time' style events, when panels of politicians, teachers and parents debated key education issues based on questions from the audience. The format was intended to have broad appeal and to open up debate about a whole host of issues that were the basis of the union's alternative (funding, assessment, governance and democracy).

Politicians (national and local) were often part of the 'Question Time' panels, and the union made a conscious decision to make sure politicians were aware of the issues the union was raising. For example, on 10 June 2014, the union organised a lobby of parliament when more than 25% of MPs received representations from teachers.

Throughout all this activity, and engagement with parents, politicians and the community, the union was clear that industrial action was a key element in its strategy and that the union would continue to take strike action, nationally and locally, as appropriate.

The NUT internal document summed up the union's 'Stand Up For Education' campaign as follows:

The Stand up for Education campaign is comprised of the following elements: professional unity; engagement with parents; pressuring politicians; taking industrial action. These strands are interrelated and reinforce each other. They attempt to both make a difference in the here and now for teachers and children, but crucially they attempt to organise members in engaging with parents, politicians and others in building a social movement around a better vision of education than that based upon competition, privatisation, high stakes testing and the de-professionalisation of teaching. The Stand up for Education campaign may have gotten rid of Michael Gove, we now need to ensure we get rid of the GERM![9]

'Stand Up For Education' was a watershed moment for the NUT. It represented a genuine attempt to implement in practice a modelled strategy that aimed to slow down, disrupt and ultimately replace the dominant neoliberal model of education. It qualitatively moved the union's campaigning and political work away from being a series of (often unconnected) tactics that, to paraphrase Sun Tzu, created noise, but would often be followed by defeat. Thousands of members had taken an active role in the campaign at a local level – organising, and taking part in hundreds of local meetings where parents and educators put would-be politicians on the spot to get them to commit to changes in the education system.

However, the changes, while inspired and often initiated by grassroots members, were largely being directed from the union's central office. Further, the new campaign focus and activity were increasingly taking place away from the workplace and the realities of everyday work as it was experienced by teachers and other education workers. As a result, members were often 'mobilised' as opposed to being 'organised', in that they were encouraged to 'do things', rather than determining for themselves what needed doing.

Also, however significant internally, the immediate and wider political impact of 'Stand Up For Education' was limited, and it is important to acknowledge this. A considerable success of the campaign was to channel the mass pressure of many members on Education Minister Michael Gove and to see him removed as Secretary of State for Education.[10] Deliberate targeting of Gove had resulted in him becoming toxic within the teaching profession, and he was clearly considered a potential electoral liability. However, the campaign did not result in a break, in any meaningful way, with neoliberalism in the education manifestos presented by the three major political parties. Also, the working lives of teachers were not improving within the education system. Indeed, the outcome of the 2015 election saw the Conservative Party elected with a majority big enough to abandon their coalition partners. This looked like unwelcome news for the NUT, and promised further fragmentation and liberalisation in education.

However, things were soon to change.

'THE MOST SUCCESSFUL TRADE UNION CAMPAIGN IN A GENERATION': THE CORRECT STRATEGY WITH EFFECTIVE TACTICS

Not long after Michael Gove's departure, his successor, Nicky Morgan, made the following statement at a major education technology convention known as *The BETT Show*:

> As we inject further choice and competition to the school system, parents and students will rightly demand more information from us so that they can exercise that choice effectively.
>
> We need to consider how the era of 'big data' can help to provide it.
>
> Already we have begun to produce destination data on school leavers to identify where they end up. We aim to include them in league tables by 2017.
>
> In future, we could try to link qualifications to tax data too in order to demonstrate the true worth of certain subjects.[11]

In this speech, there is early evidence of the government's ongoing ideological commitment to marketisation (now to be supported by the power of huge for-profit education technology companies), but also its over-confidence in its own ability to drive this agenda forward. To quote from Sun Tzu's *The Art of War*, 'The opportunity of defeating the enemy is provided by the enemy themself', and so it was to be with the political overstretch of Nicky Morgan.

By 2015, the NUT believed that it had developed an organising model that could begin to contest and transform the education landscape and the working lives of members, based on their self-activity and that of allies. What was missing was the opportunity to test this model at scale. 'Stand Up For Education' had offered tantalising glimpses of what a transformative organising approach could look like, but the goal had not been realised. The circumstances had not been right.

This was to change early in 2016, when the government set out its education policy agenda for the new parliament in a white paper titled *Education Excellence Everywhere* (*EEE*).[12] This offered the NUT the opportunity it had been waiting for. In this, Morgan proposed a number of measures to further embed the radical reform agenda initiated by Michael Gove in 2010. Under the proposals, schools would find it both easier and quicker to become an academy. Indeed, the white paper explicitly stated: 'By the end of 2020 all schools will be academies, or in the process of becoming academies. By the end of 2022, local authorities will no longer maintain schools' (p. 55). This drive to 'inject further choice and competition' (from Morgan's *BETT Show* speech) was absolutely tied to the notion that parents and pupils were consumers, and that the intrinsic value of education was about the accumulation of human capital. As the quote from Morgan above shows, the 'true worth' of an academic subject was to be measured in the wage it was likely to generate in the world of work. This was how debased English school education was becoming, and why the need to build an alternative was so critical.

The *EEE* proposals were clearly an acceleration of the existential threat to the NUT's values and ability to function effectively. However, having carefully tracked the speed and rate of academy conversion, it was also clear to the NUT that the government would struggle to deliver on its own goals. The union also recognised that the chapter in the white paper on a new school funding formula, combined with the Tories' continued commitment to austerity measures, would mean that the overwhelming majority of schools would see, often dramatic, reductions in funding, and that these reductions would disproportionately fall on schools in many inner cities with high levels of social deprivation.

In March 2016, the NUT balloted members to take strike action against the threat to terms and conditions posed by academisation and cuts in funding presented within the white paper. A resounding 91.7% voted in favour of action, but on a turnout of under 25% – a turnout that, if the ballot had of been conducted several months later after the introduction of the Trade Union Act 2016, would have fallen well short of the necessary legal threshold to take industrial action. The vote for action reflected member anger, but the low turnout highlighted the challenges of turning anger into action in a hyper-fragmented school system.

The publication of the white paper had provoked a strong reaction across all teaching unions. While the National Association of Head-teachers and the Association of School and College Leaders did not hold the same 'in principle' position against the creation of academies, they did resent the notion of compulsion. The campaigning pressure from all unions resulted in several Tory MPs and council groups speaking out against the forced mass academisation of schools. This pressure, combined with the pragmatic realisation of their overstretch, resulted in the government abandoning the proposal. As Nicky Morgan was forced to concede:

> I am today reaffirming our determination to see all schools become academies. However, having listened to the feedback from parliamentary colleagues and the education sector, we will now change the path to reaching that goal.[13]

As *The Guardian* at the time stated, this was an 'abrupt U-turn'.[14] For the first time in many years, government had been pushed back on a major question of policy.

Following the government climbdown, the national executive had to decide whether or not to progress with the planned strike action. Having won a substantial concession, the fact that the NUT would be striking without the support of any other education unions, with all the difficulties that entailed, was clearly a challenge. Combined with the fact that the end of the school term was rapidly approaching, some executive members argued that the action should not proceed. However, the NUT's general secretary, deputy general secretary and a majority of executive members were adamant that the strike needed to go ahead to act as a launch pad for the next phase of what was increasingly conceptualised as a long-term campaign orientation. A strike date of 5 July was called, and in the build-up to the strike, and on the day itself, the government attempted to portray the action as being about teachers' self-interest (terms and conditions of employment), whereas the union increasingly went on the offensive around the issue of school funding. While the strike action itself was not successful in closing a great number of schools outside NUT-dominated areas, it represented a significant victory in beginning to win public support around the issue of school funding cuts.

At the time, the Institute of Fiscal Studies noted that the government's funding plans would amount to an 8% real-terms cut in school funding across the duration of the parliament. However, talk of 'billions of pounds' and percentages often lessens the impact on the public imagination. Understanding the direct impact on individual schools is far harder-hitting, so it was the NUT's good fortune that the division secretary in Camden, a vocal supporter of the NUT's turn to organising, used his detailed understanding of 'big data' to construct a funding modeller that accurately showed for every school in England the level of cuts they faced. This understanding and use of data were the foundation stone of the NUT's 'School Cuts' campaign.

Throughout the autumn of 2016, the Camden division secretary – who would be become a NUT staff member during the campaign – worked with Outlandish, a team of socially progressive web developers, and The Small Axe, a campaigns company rooted in wanting to make a positive change in society, to construct a campaign website and associated social media strategy. The website showed, via a postcode search function, every school in England and the level of cuts each school faced. Figures were translated into the actual impact this could have, equating how many fewer teachers would be employed, for example. More than statistics alone, the campaign was based on speaking through the experience of education workers and parents. Broaching new territory for the union, targeted social media adverts were commissioned, and proved highly effective in reaching the hoped-for audience.

The website and campaign increasingly acted as an organiser and inspiration for the various local, often parent-led, anti-cuts campaigns that were starting to spring up around the country. The great weakness of the government's position was that its denial of cuts and its mantra of a fairer distribution of monies ran up against the real-life lived experience of head teachers often having to send letters to parents asking for money to plug funding gaps, and of parents recognising that the education offer available to their children was being eroded. In this way, the 'common sense' of the government's austerity and neoliberal reform agenda began to crack in a fundamental way, with the NUT playing the leading role in both breaking the hegemony and building the movement that forced the government on the defensive. The union was playing a decisive role in opening up cracks in the government's neoliberal reform process and driving wedges into the divisions that were emerging.

What gave the 'School Cuts' campaign real momentum was the snap election called by Theresa May for 8 June 2017. When this was announced during the NUT national conference, the union immediately went on the front foot, sensing an opportunity to build the campaign around funding and engage with and pressure opposition parties around a broader set of ideas for education. This opportunity had been magnified by the election of Jeremy Corbyn as leader of the Labour Party and the party's subsequent commitment to building a National Education Service (NES) that promised cradle-to-grave education opportunities as a social good as well as providing people with the skills required for participation in the labour market.[15] While the details of the NES remained vague, the emergence of the NES onto the policy agenda created new opportunities for the NUT and its vision of a radical alternative to the prevailing system.

At a tactical level, the campaign focus shifted to directly engage with the election. The campaign website was pivotal to the project, and was updated with new features that created compelling ways for the public to engage and become active around the issue of funding during the general election campaign. The key feature was to allow people to make direct contact with their prospective MP via the website and request they pledge to fight funding cuts if elected. The website also showed responses from candidates, making clear whether the candidates in their constituency had pledged to fight school cuts.

A further feature was an analysis of spending pledges for each political party that displayed in a simple and clear format how Conservative, Labour and Liberal Democrat manifesto commitments would affect all schools in England.

Finally, in order to help develop grassroots activity, the website allowed individuals to print their own materials to be handed out to parents at the school gates and in the wider community. More than this, the website allowed individuals, schools, parents groups and even local authorities to order campaign materials *en masse* for free. Hundreds of thousands of tailored leaflets, posters and banners were ordered during the election campaign. The NUT spent a total of £326,000 during the election,[16] making it one of the highest-spending 'third parties' in the election, much to the ire of a number of Conservative MPs.

The BBC journalist Chris Cooke posed the rhetorical question on social media: 'is the NUT's campaign against school cuts the most effective union campaign in decades?'[17] The campaign was undoubtedly successful in raising the issue of funding cuts. By the time election day came round, the issue polled as the third most important issue for all voters, and was responsible for 750,000 people changing their voting intentions.[18] This clearly helped Labour the most – the combination of showing that cuts were real and Labour's promise of a fully funded National Education Service had affected real-world politics.

While the Tories were elected on a much smaller majority than anticipated, after the election they continued to deny the reality of the school cuts. However, it was becoming increasingly clear that their hegemony within education policy was beginning to crack. Labour, the Liberal Democrats and the Greens not only accepted the reality of cuts, but all pledged, to varying degrees, to commit to significant investment in education. More than this, for the first time in several decades, mainstream political parties were offering education manifestos that broke with the central tenets of neoliberal education policy. Standardised testing, league tables, outdated GCSE exams and the punitive regulator Ofsted would all be abandoned, according to the Greens, Liberal Democrats and Labour. While it would be hubristic to claim that the NUT's campaigning was alone responsible for this movement, it would also be a denial of fact to say that the union was not an important agent in this process of change. The success of 'School Cuts' was not just at the level of campaign *tactics* (the use of data, the campaign website, the use of social media etc.), the tactics were in pursuance of a *strategy* that had been developed over several years. It was this combination of strategy *and* tactics that resulted in not just winning the ideological and political argument around funding, but also opening up a space where wider arguments could be had about a different model of education and the role of teachers within this. In other words, it helped develop the building of a counter-hegemonic movement. The funding campaign brought together other teaching and support staff unions as well as various parents' groups, and by working together, more generalised discussions about the future of education developed. Building on this success, and these embryonic alliances, was to play a significant role in the early months of the newly formed National Education Union.

In the two short years since the launch of 'Stand Up For Education', the NUT had made considerable strategic progress: amalgamation with the Association of Teachers and Lecturers (ATL); a demonstrated ability to build genuine alliances with parents and other campaign and civil society groups; the ability to influence national politics and pressure lawmakers of various political stripes. In short, the goal of creating a counter-hegemonic movement was seen to be possible. What was less clear was how this movement connected with the union at its base. While democratically agreed, and regularly reported to the national executive, the strategy depended heavily on direction from the union's central office, and this remained an ongoing problem. Despite efforts to facilitate and encourage activity, it was still the case, as the NUT ceased to exist in August 2017, that there was still no rank-and-file revival as had been witnessed in Chicago, and which was developing elsewhere in the

United States. The number of members involved in campaigns was not as high as it needed to be, and fundamentally, the working lives of teachers were not improving. Moreover, the union was struggling to integrate key issues, such as those relating to sex and race oppression, into the core of its activity. This was highlighted when the union commissioned and published a research report on sexism in schools titled *It's Just Everywhere*[19] (based on the words of one student describing the prevalence of sexism in her school). The report offered an excoriating, research-based critique of the sexist nature of the education system and the extraordinary levels of sexism and harassment that girls and women within it were experiencing. As such, it represented a direct ideological challenge to the normalising of oppression and harassment which the report described as 'endemic but not inevitable'. The research contained many powerful recommendations and suggestions for action, and there are several examples where union members have worked with the report to drive change in their schools and colleges. Ultimately, however, the work remained disconnected from the union's wider campaigning, and nor was it embedded in the type of campaign model described in this chapter. As such, it has arguably failed to secure the impact that the report itself demonstrated is so necessary. What this example highlights is the need to locate strategic priorities within a coherent campaign model, but also the need for such a model to connect campaigns so that core concerns are not marginalised and broad alliances can be developed. As the new union was formed, these became increasingly important issues.

THE NATIONAL EDUCATION UNION: 'OUR AIM IS TO SHAPE THE FUTURE OF EDUCATION'

Throughout the 1990s and 2000s, the trade union movement witnessed several important mergers and amalgamations. This strategy was seen by some as a way of countering membership decline and a loss of bargaining strength. Removing competition – in sectors and individual workplaces – between unions is clearly something to be welcomed, but it will only work as an effective strategy if there is then a positive approach to how the new union uses its extra membership and potential increased strength. In many cases in the UK, mergers and amalgamations have been measured on financial metrics of efficiency and economies of scale. As Roger Undy (2008) has noted, many of the union mergers of the past several decades have ultimately resulted in membership decline. Research studies have also observed that unions which have gone through this process often become bogged down in internal reorganisation, at both staff and lay level, which results in the organisations looking inward so that any increased workplace or sectoral strength are often squandered.

It was with this knowledge in mind that from the outset of the National Education Union's formation there was a conscious effort to try to keep the focus of the amalgamation on the outside world. The NUT had as a long-standing principle that there should be one union for education workers. In a sector with high density, there was a clear logic to this position. The NUT entered the amalgamation with the ATL with a rising membership and, more unevenly, an activist base. The ATL, while not growing in membership numbers, was a large, viable organisation with no financial imperative to amalgamate. The amalgamation was therefore one of principle rather than necessity, brokered over several years. This can be seen in the way in which, rather than the smaller union merging into the larger, the bringing together of the two legacy unions would result in a new formation. Further, the new union would be led by joint general secretaries for the first five years of its existence – Mary Bousted, General Secretary of the ATL, and Kevin Courtney, General Secretary of the NUT. Likewise, structural guarantees were given to ensure representation of former ATL members on the national executive and in the new local structures.[20]

Unlike the NUT, the ATL's membership included school support staff, and this was also to be the case in the NEU. This opened the opportunity for the new union to adopt a 'wall-to-wall' approach to its organising work and increase its industrial strength in workplaces. The building of solidarity between teaching and support staff, and between the NUT and ATL in the run-up to amalgamation, was seen in a dispute between teaching assistants across County Durham and the local authority in 2016. This dispute also showed how workers (overwhelmingly women) who were often overlooked and previously not seen as a focus of systematic organising work could become a powerful force and throw up a layer of new workplace leaders.

While the NEU is not recognised at a national level by support staff employers for the purpose of collective bargaining, at a local level this lack of formal recognition has been overcome by organising support staff around issues central to them in the workplace. Importantly for the

NEU, support staff are often more rooted in their local community than teachers who often live outside of the community they serve. The potential of a union comprising both teachers and support staff, with the latter rooted in their communities, would be key to how the NEU's organising and campaigns approach was conceptualised.

At its launch in January 2017, the NEU mission statement read: 'our aim is to shape the future of education'. Such a bold statement acted as an orientation point for the new union. An internal document stated clearly that a new campaigning approach, to supplement organising work, would be needed:

> The primary function of the NEU campaigns is to make a significant contribution to fulfilling the NEU's mission statement, by developing and delivering *strategic campaigns* that seek to build the power and influence of the NEU. This power and influence will be used to effect positive change and better position the union to have a voice in schools and colleges, as well as with policy makers, in the short, medium and long term. NEU campaigns are about making change happen – by incremental gains and qualitative successes. In demonstrating the effectiveness of the NEU, campaigns will contribute to the growth and prestige of the union.[21]

However, the new union immediately recognised that the effectiveness of its campaigns could not be secured by advocacy alone, but that it was necessary to build union power in order to secure the leverage required to bring about change. The document went on to assert:

> Leverage can result from strength of argument, quality of research, the ability to communicate effectively, and – crucially – the ability to mobilise collective opinion, strength and activity around issues of importance. NEU campaigns should offer access points at multiple levels for membership engagement and participation in line with the NEU's organising method. Beyond this, NEU campaigns should constantly seek to identify external allies and stakeholders to work with around agreed aims.[22]

Building on the hegemonic model developed in the NUT, which described a *method* of operation, it was thought necessary to show in clear terms both the aspiration of the new union and how struggling for system change would lead to day-to-day victories. In other words, there was a relationship between both the quantity and quality of activity, not just an exhortation for 'more'. The purpose of this was to lift the aspiration of the union, but not to sound as if the union's work was demanding the impossible. It was important that the campaign work of the union was based on an acceptance of the world as it was, and not as union activists might want it to be, and furthermore, that multiple entry points into activity were offered to members and allies. The NEU was to be *realistic* and *radical*. It was to have an optimism of the will, albeit tempered with a pessimism of the intellect.

A starting point of this 'radical realism' was to look at what constituted the key components of neoliberal reform that had the greatest negative impact upon both the working lives of members but also were at odds with the union's principled view of education. Rather than just respond to 'this and this', the NEU would pick the territory it would fight on. That is not to say these would be the only areas that the union would campaign around, but they would take priority in terms of effort and resources. These areas would be strategic, in the sense that a victory in any one of them would be a setback for the entire neoliberal reform movement. The areas of strategic focus were school funding, assessment and accountability, and child poverty. Each campaign area allowed activity at an industrial, political and ideological level; the activity could be conducted locally and nationally, and the building of alliances was crucial to all.

Each of these areas would also have a campaign framework to work to. While in and of themselves they could not be described as original, these frameworks had not been used in either legacy union of the NEU. This was a new approach for the NEU, and was evidence of the new union establishing its own distinctive ways of working. The importance of these frameworks was to ensure that there was clarity in *what* each campaign was trying to achieve and *how* the union would go about achieving it. In doing so, these frameworks ensured that strategy and tactics were not misunderstood or confused, that tactics were always informed by strategy, and that there was clear-sightedness on the target of the campaign. The union established a template to help frame each campaign and to maximise the potential for impact (see box overleaf).

Campaigns would be measured on five-year cycles – from one general election to another. Governments could be persuaded or forced to act

Define aims: *What are we trying to achieve?*
- How big is the gap between where we are and where we would like to be? This will give a sense of scope, timescales, and resources needed to succeed.

Define target: Who is the decision-maker, what are their strengths and weaknesses, and what is our 'ask' of them?

Strategy:
- How do we build our power, leverage and influence on the target?
- How do we weaken the power, influence and arguments of the campaign target?

Campaign narrative: Creating a vision of necessary change
- What's wrong with current situation?
- What will be better if we are successful?
- How we are going to win?

Tactics: What, how and where we are active to help us achieve our strategy of building our power and leverage, and weakening our campaign target.

before elections, but as education policy is in the hands of national government, working within election cycles offered a useful framework for planning longer-term strategy.

The new union had developed a sophisticated organising model and campaigns framework – but would it be enough to rise to the challenge?

ARE WE WINNING YET? THE LIMITS OF CAMPAIGNING WITHOUT SYSTEMATIC MEMBER PARTICIPATION

For those wanting to bring about fundamental change in society, the key question to constantly reflect on is what progress is being made. Any assessment needs to be honest and open. Exaggerating success may lead to a misunderstanding of the balance of forces and result in wrong strategic decisions being made. Conversely, not recognising success and progress can also lead to poor strategic choices, as well as creating a sense of inertia and demoralisation. So, drawing up an honest balance sheet, what progress did the NEU make in its first years of existence in its attempt to break the hegemonic grip of neoliberal policy?

'School Cuts' scored a major victory prior to the 2019 general election. After numerous attacks, denials that cuts were happening, and complaints that the union was misleading the public, the Conservative government of Boris Johnson committed to plug the funding hole left by austerity. This was undoubtedly because the government wanted to kill the issue prior to the 2019 general election, even though this would be an election clearly dominated by Brexit. The government also announced prior to the election that the starting salaries of newly qualified teachers would increase to £30,000. While the COVID-19 pandemic would put these gains into question, it is undoubtedly the case that the NEU-led campaign had forced the government to backtrack on a decade-long trajectory.

On the issue of assessment, the situation is more complex. The More Than A Score coalition group (launched in the days of the NUT to campaign against standardised testing in primary schools) grew in both the depth and breadth of its support. Making gains in working with wider groups of parents and school leaders outside the NEU, on several occasions the coalition delayed the introduction of a new standardised test for 4-year-olds. At a political level, in the 2019 general election the Conservatives were the only party that pledged to keep Ofsted and high-stakes testing in place. And even within the Conservative Party, cracks were beginning to show on these issues. However, it would not be until the COVID-19 pandemic shone a harsh light on the fault lines in both primary and secondary assessment in England that the NEU's assessment work began to reach a wide layer of parents who were suddenly exposed to the faults in the system of assessment.

So, across the strategic campaign areas, *quantitative progress* could be demonstrated in trying to achieve *qualitative change*, using an agreed campaign model, and sticking with agreed frameworks. But there was an undeniable problem. While many members were engaged, too few were consistently involved in union campaigns, and if one believes that people need to be active in trying to change the world around them to change their consciousness, then this remains a fundamental issue. Change was still, to a large degree, dependent on national office initiatives, alongside a relatively small layer of activists. The mass of union members were not systematically involved, and where they were, they were often mobilised, and not organised in the sense used by Jane McAlevey and discussed in Chapter 2. Another undeniable fact is that whatever the successes to the counter-hegemonic struggle, the day-to-day lives of teachers were not improving. Indeed, an unintended consequence of the relative success of the NEU campaigns was that they often impacted on its organising efforts in schools.

The emphasis within the campaigns strategy on defining the government as the target to be pressured highlighted an underlying issue within the orientation of the NEU that itself is a reflection of a tension within the education system. Individual schools have a high degree of autonomy, but this autonomy is only allowed within a rigid, centralised system. School leaders can, and do, make decisions that impact on individuals and collective staff bodies, but the power of a school leader is not limitless. This contradiction, and the challenge to the NEU of getting the balance right between campaigning to change the system while dealing with its day-to-day consequences, is best illustrated by the issue of workload.

Workload is consistently the number one issue of concern for teachers. It is what drives teachers from the profession. Teachers' frustration with unsustainable working hours is clearly a major problem, but so is the lack of control teachers feel they have over their own work. Organising to press school leaders to alleviate workload problems is clearly possible and necessary, but the pressure within a system based on competition will constantly push back against any gains made locally. Therefore, there is a need to mount a fundamental challenge to the wider system which is about more than an ongoing attritional fight and sees system change as part of a longer-term process. In such a campaign, however, what is the correct balance between organising and campaigning, between the national and local? The potential answers to these questions were presented to the union in the most dramatic and unforeseen way during the COVID-19 pandemic.

6

Organising in a Crisis

We defeated a government. We were the opposition. Where the
[official] Opposition should have been, the NEU were the opposition.
(John, NEU workplace rep[1])

INTRODUCTION

In January 2020, it was clear that significant issues confronted the
newly formed National Education Union. At the time, membership was
falling, which is a pattern that can often follow a union merger or amalgamation. However, there was also a sense that some trends were more
fundamental and challenging. For example, the chronic teacher retention problems in England, caused by unsustainable workloads and poor
pay, were inevitably impacting union membership. Furthermore, changes
in teacher training, including increased 'on the job' school-based routes
into teaching, were denying the union access to traditional opportunities to recruit new members.[2] Moreover, it also appeared that the union
was struggling to maintain rep density in schools, despite all its focus on
workplace organising. Finally, it is important to note that the union had
conducted two national indicative ballots,[3] one on pay in December 2018
and the other on a proposed boycott of standardised testing in primary
schools in June 2019, and that both ballots had failed to demonstrate
levels of member support that made a campaign of industrial action on
either issue possible, let alone have a strong chance of delivering a victory.

Within 12 months, the situation above was transformed as the impact
of the Coronavirus pandemic redefined the context in which trade
unions were organising. By January 2021, the union had gained 50,000
new members,[4] many of whom were young, and had recruited more than
4,500 new workplace reps, significantly increasing the number of Black
and LGBT+ reps. Seven in ten of the new reps were women. Much of the
membership growth was among support staff, who are a sector of the

education workforce that are the most vulnerable and exploited. They are overwhelmingly women and disproportionately Black workers.

During the same period, educators inflicted numerous defeats on government, making schools, students and communities safer in the process. This included the moment when the union forced the government into an unprecedented U-turn, ensuring that it reversed its commitment to fully open schools for the start of the 2021 calendar year (referred to in Chapter 1). Tory MPs, various right-wing pressure groups and sections of the media were incandescent with rage, accusing the union of 'playing politics' and 'hijacking the pandemic'[5] to demand pay rises, while the union calmly maintained it was acting in the best interests of members, children and school communities. The government had been isolated and exposed, and was forced to retreat.

The events of January 2021 were not the result of any isolated decision by the union, but were the direct consequence of the NEU and NUT's organising and campaigning activity over a period of more than a decade, and that has been described in the two previous chapters. As a result of this work, the union was able to assert a leading role politically and ideologically, as well as industrially, at a crucial moment in time. January 2021 was not the result of serendipity, and it certainly was not a fluke, but rather it was the result of conscious leadership in the union over a sustained period.

COVID-19 transformed the context and created the conditions for the NEU's workplace organising and political campaigning to come together in a way that had only been hinted at previously. Such a powerful alignment of these two strategies, combined with effective and emergent leadership at multiple levels of the union, demonstrated what is possible when grassroots organising integrates industrial and political dimensions with explicit ideological struggle.

THE PANDEMIC STRIKES: THE CONTEXT REDEFINED

On 16 March 2020, Prime Minister Boris Johnson announced that people should avoid non-essential contact, and on 23 March he pronounced that everyone should 'stay at home', effectively introducing a national lockdown. Despite this exhortation, schools were exempt from a complete lockdown, and immediately became a site of struggle between those prioritising health and safety concerns and those prioritising economic interests.

In response, the NEU advised members at greater risk, or living with those at greater risk, to cease attending work from the following Monday, and advised school leaders to use their professional judgement on whether to open schools and colleges. The NEU's joint general secretaries wrote directly to Boris Johnson, stating:

> Given the number of staff and pupils that will now be off school, teachers and leaders will simply have to exercise their professional discretion about whether schools and colleges open and what work is undertaken – *and they should do so with your approval.*
> We will support them in so doing.[6]

Within 24 hours, the government had made its first U-turn of the pandemic and most teaching was moved online. Schools remained open to teach at-risk students and the children of key workers, and in the words of the NEU press release, educators were 'willing to volunteer' to staff this provision. From the outset, it was clear that individual schools were the key frontier of control and that the consent of educators could no longer be taken for granted. The state could make national pronouncements about broad policy, but it was in individual schools where decisions would be made about rotas for face-to-face teaching, where health and safety protocols were drawn up and where expectations about how online learning might be conducted were determined. It was clear from the outset that union reps in schools would be on the front line.

This collective action by union members was in response to an unprecedented context. Not only did the pandemic cause dramatic changes to the work of school staff, at a moment's notice and without any adequate resourcing, but the simple act of going to work had become a potential life-and-death matter. Many school leaders were very supportive, or tried to be as supportive as policy allowed them to be, but many staff realised that their health and safety often came second to other priorities. The system simply did not care about them. This was also the moment when staff realised that if they acted individually, they were powerless and easily picked off.

This was a decisive moment when the consciousness of school staff shifted. Perhaps tentatively and incoherently, but it was a moment when many school staff understood the need to act collectively, and that the union was the vehicle for such action. Staff who had never been in the union joined in their thousands, while huge numbers of previously passive members became much more engaged in union activities, searching for union advice, but also connecting with fellow members in their workplace to put their demands to management. In short, they began to *act collectively*.

One young teacher from London described the experience in the following terms:

> The pandemic has politicised educators on a mass scale. They are beginning to recognise the purpose of a union to protect and act as a collective voice for change. We have strength in numbers.

The NEU was well placed to support this surge in workplace activity, because it built on the workplace organising described previously. One initial response was to redeploy large numbers of NEU staff to have a direct conversation with every workplace rep in the country, so that reps in schools felt supported and connected to the union. This was an extraordinary and unprecedented response by the union, and while clearly driven from head office, showed a determination to place workplace reps at the centre of the union's response to the crisis.

The union also actively sought to recruit reps where schools had no rep and quickly created the role of 'COVID rep' as a way of drawing members more easily into union action. COVID reps were recruited on the basis that they specifically negotiated COVID-related issues in their school, but the hope was that these reps would ultimately take on a more wide-ranging and permanent role as workplace reps.

By May 2020, it became clear that the government intended to instigate a wider opening of schools on 1 June, more rapidly than scientific experts were advising, and that this could pose a significant risk to life. Based on scientific advice from Independent SAGE,[7] the union publicly launched its 'Five Tests' campaign that set out the union's minimum expectations for safe working. It declared that in-person education should not resume unless and until these were met.

Once again, the union responded by reaching out directly to its members and giving them concrete actions to take at workplace level. Workplace reps and the new COVID reps were provided with model letters for the management in their schools, stating that staff would not return to work until their union said it was safe to do so. They asked all staff (not just union members) to sign these before forwarding them to their headteachers. Similar letters were produced at local authority level, to be signed by all workplace reps.

This initiative emerged from discussions among grassroots activists within the union, and was intended to function as a structure test to establish member willingness to take collective action. The initiative was then taken up and implemented by the union nationally alongside online health and safety checklists (produced alongside other education sector unions, including Unite, Unison and the GMB) which allowed workplace groups to rate preparations for a safe return to work at their school/college. An online checklist app was developed rapidly, and encouraged workplace reps to submit data in real time to branch secretaries, regional offices and the union headquarters, allowing the union to make an immediate assessment of the state of play in workplaces across the country. In this way, digital technology was used not just to add additional weight in the form of online petitions or other actions, but to directly stimulate and measure real-world collective action. This was not technology as a source of largely passive 'clicktivism', but rather technology as an essential support to grassroots organising in workplaces.

Once again, the intention was to ensure that it was NEU workplace reps who were negotiating directly with management about the provisions which needed to be in place for wider opening, and to delay the process, in order to reduce the risk to life. It made the response real in the workplace and put the power in the hands of workplace groups. It required a level of workplace organising and negotiating on a scale not seen since 1984–1986. One school rep described her experience:

In my own school we had built a WhatsApp group and were sharing information and being critical of our own school's planning throughout. We got together and used the union checklist to ensure that our own workplace was as safe as possible and raised any issues we had.

In another instance, a workplace rep illustrated exactly what was described in Chapter 4 as the 'virtuous circle of workplace organisation':

From the get-go, we knew we were going to be organised because we are an organised group. As members in school, we are constantly in contact, and I was getting phone calls to the classroom and people wandering up saying, is something going to be done? … We had a union meeting immediately and fed back to the head the next day. We spoke as a group about how we were going to approach it.

When 1 June came round, there was no central government U-turn, but rather individual schools, academy trusts and local authorities simply refused to follow government plans for wider opening, and instead looked to work with their school union groups to agree concrete and safe plans for the wider re-opening. In the majority of cases, opening was delayed by two weeks or more, significantly reducing the risk of infection, hospitalisations and possible fatalities.

For the second time, the NEU could realistically say that its actions had prevented countless unnecessary infections, and ultimately deaths.

When schools re-opened for the new academic year in September 2020, it was clear that the COVID crisis was still shaping everyone's lives. This was a long way from Boris Johnson's risible claim in March 2020 that the UK could 'turn the tide' on the pandemic in 12 weeks.[8] Schools continued to have to work with inadequate resources, chaotic planning and a 'command and control' approach to policy that refused to engage with those actually trying to make schools work in a public health crisis.

As the winter approached, it rapidly became obvious that COVID transmission rates would rise again, and by late September new restrictions were introduced by government. By early November, a second national lockdown was in place, but the government insisted on omitting schools from the new requirements.

As the end of the autumn term in 2020 approached, a new strain of COVID (Delta) began to spread and rates were climbing significantly, in London especially. Early signs of government's refusal to react were evident when it threatened court action against some London local authorities that proposed early closures before the end of term. The government was adamant that before and after the holiday period, schools would continue largely as 'normal'. For some time, it had been increasingly clear that such an approach was reckless, and that when schools re-opened in the new year, transmission rates would rise to dangerous levels.

Since around October, some in the union had been calling for a national strike over health and safety, but opinion on this issue was divided, even among the activist base. There was a significant danger that an industrial action ballot would have proved unsuccessful in the context of the UK's legal requirements for strike ballots, and would therefore have undermined the union's position. It was clear a more flexible and responsive strategy was required given the rapidly changing context.

In late December, the situation began to change dramatically. On 30 December, in the middle of the holiday period, a meeting of over 500 activists, organised by local officers, called for a delayed return, and grassroots members demanded 'No January return until it is safe'.[9] The following day, the advice of the government's own expert panel (which had been presented to the government two weeks previously[10]) was released, and it became apparent that the government was proceeding with re-opening schools against the advice of its own scientific advisers.

Informal discussions took place immediately within the union, and an emergency National Executive meeting was set for Saturday 2 January, to be followed by an online members' meeting on Sunday 3 January, the day before schools were set to return.

After two hours of debate, the National Executive voted unanimously to advise all members that it was not safe to return to work and that it was the considered opinion of the union that they should exercise their rights under Section 44 of the Health and Safety at Work Act not to enter an unsafe workplace.

Model letters were immediately issued to members to help them communicate their intention not to engage in on-site working. At the same time, members were invited to take part in an online meeting the following day. Around 70,000 members logged in to the meeting directly on Zoom, and another 400,000 watched the meeting online.

The outcome was that 'Section 44 letters' were submitted to headteachers by tens of thousands of school staff, and the majority of schools and colleges announced that they would not be opening on Monday 4 January. That same evening, in a national TV broadcast, the prime minister acknowledged that schools and colleges were 'vectors of transmission'[11] and would remain closed to prevent the spread of the virus, with partial opening for at-risk students and the children of key workers as previously.

One rep described the impact that this chain of events had on them and their members, starting from the December activist meeting:

It was the best meeting I have ever been to …. People were angry, people were passionate, people were going to use Section 44. And then literally a day or two later, Mary and Kevin (I'm guessing they heard what was said – they must have done) turned round and said, 'Alright, we'll back you on this,' and said it nationally to everyone. 'If you don't want to go in to work, use Section 44. We'll back you.' That was an incredible, powerful moment – going from that meeting to Mary and Kevin, and then Boris Johnson basically saying, 'I'm shutting schools.'

That moment showed that we had the power to actually push back on the government and make them make a different decision. That was a wonderful moment.

Another rep described the way in which workplace organising and solidarity created the conditions in which members felt able to push back.

It was really positive because we knew we were taking this step and we were being told we would save lives by doing this. At the same time, it was frightening because we felt that, although it wasn't actually industrial action, we were putting our neck on the line. We were prepared to stand up for something that we were a little bit scared of really … but all of us were together, and we kept checking in with each other.

Us organising in schools gives members the confidence that the bigger things can be achieved.

The government's U-turn in January 2021 was achieved because of the mass mobilisation of workplace reps who were able to organise collective action by members in schools in a way that forced the government into retreat. The union made significant use of technology throughout this period, including developing new digital organising tools, but this was always to facilitate and support real-world organising in the workplace. During the pandemic, the number of reps had increased considerably, and the nature of the public health crisis had encouraged a level of activism and militancy that had not been evident for some time. All of this activity built on an intentional strategy of developing workplace organisation that had been in place for over a decade. This type of union-building was the foundation on which the success in January 2021 was based, and provides a platform for further grassroots organising.

However, and importantly, it was also only one part of the story, because the union's workplace organising on health and safety issues also took place in a wider political and ideological context around the immediate problems facing schools, but also much wider questions about what the future of education should look like.

BREAKING THE NEOLIBERAL HEGEMONY: ORGANISING AROUND AN ALTERNATIVE

From the outset, it was clear that right-wing politicians and the media would pose the debate about school openings in populist terms, invoking their own well-worn stereotypes that equated schools being 'closed' (which they were not) with teachers sitting at home with their feet up and a cup of coffee. The challenge for the union, therefore, was to confront such narratives and reframe the issues in ways that emphasised health and safety concerns and the prioritising of people's health over economic imperatives. The union had understood from the very start of the pandemic that the government would not engage seriously with the teaching profession about its COVID plans for schools, and it certainly would not engage with the NEU. Hence the union recognised the need to treat its own intervention as part of a political campaign that needed to win allies well beyond the education workforce (for a discussion of this, see Stevenson et al., 2020).

From its inception, the union's approach to COVID was firstly to focus relentlessly on the published science, and secondly to articulate health and safety concerns in relation to staff, students and local communities. Despite all the efforts of the press to present the union as only concerned with protecting the interests of its own members, the union itself made sure that all its communications emphasised a much wider set of interests, often highlighting that when schools acted as 'vectors of transmission', it was the most deprived communities, with the most poverty and the worst housing, that experienced the highest transmission rates.

The NEU's efforts to frame this narrative emerged most clearly in June 2020, when the union published a *Recovery Plan*[12] that was focused on ensuring the safe re-opening of schools, but also the steps necessary to support students in the longer term following the disruption of the initial lockdown. The NEU's *Recovery Plan* made an important intervention in the debate about schools' handling of the COVID crisis, and the support they required to build back safely and sustainably in the longer term.

However, as the public health crisis deepened, and at the same time laid bare the huge structural crises at the heart of public education (inadequate funding, the young people's mental health crisis, grotesque inequalities based on race and class), the ten-point plan also offered a more ambitious prospectus for change. Recognising that the Coronavirus crisis was obviously a threat to public health, but also an opportunity to radically reimagine the future, the NEU made the case for a public education service that not only included bold policies relating to schools (including reform of assessment and examination systems), but also demands to address wider questions of child poverty and welfare reform. These immediately connected with the experiences of many educators. For example, one teacher made the following observation:

> The pandemic has been really politicising. Doing online learning has given me such an insight into the experiences of my kids in their homes – and the huge inequalities you see.

In January 2021, as the crisis had deepened, the NEU updated and relaunched its *Education Recovery Plan*[13] organised around three clear themes:

1. safety in our schools and colleges
2. let's build a better education system
3. work as a nation to give all children and young people the best start in life

The importance of the plan was its obvious focus on addressing immediate concerns (the safe return to schools), but also its role in articulating an alternative vision of education that was very different to that of the post-

1988 neoliberal marketised model. Forced changes to the testing and exams system, and to inspection arrangements, opened up new possibilities for thinking about alternatives, and the NEU's *Recovery Plan* tapped into teachers' experiences of these changed arrangements. The plan also unequivocally highlighted the problems of child poverty:

> The last section of the plan looks beyond schools and colleges to wider societal issues, in particular the huge and lasting damage that child poverty wreaks upon our already most disadvantaged and vulnerable children and young people, and proposes concrete measures to tackle it.

The NEU's focus on child poverty intentionally highlighted structural inequalities in society that blight many young people's lives. One consequence of the pandemic was to expose these inequalities much more clearly with, for example, transmission rates (and therefore mortality rates) being substantially higher in poorer, often predominantly Black and minority ethnic, communities. Furthermore, Black workers were much more likely to be concentrated in front-line key worker roles (in social care, health, public transport and education) and so were doubly exposed to the virus – both in their homes and at work. These concerns soon emerged in the NEU as Black members demanded the union recognise the heightened risks they were being exposed to in their workplaces. This self-organising by Black members was highly significant in its own right, but also coincided with the growth of the Black Lives Matter (BLM) movement that exploded into activity following the racist murder of George Floyd by police in May 2020 in Minneapolis. At the time, a number of NEU local branches were involved in the BLM movement, and activists across the union (in particular those involved in the union's Black members' structures) immediately called for the union to take a proactive stance not only against police violence, but also for decolonisation of the curriculum and challenging structural and institutional racism within the education system (most obviously evidenced by the data relating to school exclusions, which expose a systemic problem that has gone unaddressed for decades).

The calls from branches and members were taken up nationally, both through staffing and lay structures, and in June 2020 the union held a national Zoom event with Jesse Jackson as the keynote speaker.

This event was built as an organising event and attended by thousands. Immediately following the event, the union recruited 200 new workplace reps. Centrally, staff and senior lay members began work on the *NEU Anti-racism Charter*, which was 'designed to help … explore ideas around race equality and plan how to tackle racism with children, young people and staff'.[14] This represented a significant development in the union's work on challenging racism, in particular in the curriculum, but based on a model where the school community were to take a lead in identifying and challenging issues. The model underpinning the charter represented a clear intent on the part of the union to connect central campaigns with real activity driven, and led, at the level of the workplace. At this stage, it is difficult to assess its impact. As with many similar initiatives, and highlighting a theme that is recurrent in this book, the challenge is to create an organic link between those on the ground, working in schools and communities, and the resources of the union organisation that are crucial to both supporting local activity and securing impact at a regional or national level. However, all this activity speaks to the importance of alliance-building within and beyond the union that connects immediate struggles (in this case, over health and safety at work) with wider political demands (such as those articulated by the BLM movement). In doing so, it is important to recognise that alliance-building of the type we are discussing is easy to call for in the abstract, but often difficult to construct in reality.

One practical illustration of the complexity of these types of relationships (between local and national structures, between lay-led and staff organising, between those inside and outside the union) emerged during the pandemic through several NEU initiatives focused on the impact of child poverty. For example, in January 2021 in the London Borough of Croydon, the local NEU branch funded, collated and distributed 500 'remote learning packs' to 18 schools to support children working from home and without basic resources to participate in their online classes. Local union officers co-ordinated the initiative, working with local school reps to get the packs into schools and into the hands of the children who most needed this support.

Philipa Harvey, the branch's women's officer, was reported in the local press as saying:

The idea started off for just a few children, but when we brought the idea to the [local] NEU, they said it was something they could definitely support us with, as they recognised the levels of poverty were so bad.[15]

The Croydon initiative highlights the possibilities when local union activists, building on the network of reps in schools, engage in active community organising, linking the concerns of union members with a wider set of concerns about basic access to education and the need for fully funded education and welfare provision. The momentum for the project came from activists within the Croydon branch, but it also resonated with the broader campaign being waged by the union at a national level to highlight how COVID was both impacting and exposing child poverty and its consequences for children's life chances. For example, in the same month when Croydon NEU members were distributing remote learning packs, the national NEU launched a campaign alongside the *Daily Mirror* (one of the UK's biggest tabloid newspapers) with the strapline 'Help a Child to Learn.'[16] The campaign was framed around a financial appeal (which the union kick-started with a donation of £1 million) intended to provide essential learning materials for students unable to study at home due to a lack of resources. The campaign provided essential support to students, but it also served to highlight the problems of child poverty, expose the utter inadequacy of the government's response, and also demonstrate very practically the solidarity between a trade union and the wider working-class community. The appeal was launched by the national union, but also received support from local NEU branches and individual members. It was one example of a series of initiatives, including working alongside the Manchester United footballer and free school meals campaigner Marcus Rashford,[17] that placed the union in the forefront of the campaign to tackle child poverty. As such it built directly off the 'Stand Up For Education' and 'Schools Cuts' campaigns in which the union had always linked issues of school funding to wider questions of public education and the need to tackle the structural inequalities in society that blight the lives of working-class children and those who experience intersecting oppression and discrimination based on class, race, sex, (dis)ability and sexual orientation.

The success of these campaigns was evident in the number of times the government was forced to U-turn in relation to either school closures or providing financial support to children in poverty. The campaigns were central to shifting popular thinking about the government's response to the pandemic from one of claimed competence (almost exclusively framed in relation to vaccine development) to one of obvious incompetence. So effective was this that the secretary of state for education became the focus of popular derision,[18] symbolising the inadequacy and ineffectiveness of government responses to the COVID crisis more generally.

Our view is that this political and ideological element of the NEU's campaign was essential to much of what the union achieved during the period of the pandemic when Tory politicians visibly panicked at the obvious influence of the union. These were very real achievements, and arguably represent some of the most significant victories by any union during this period. However, it is also necessary to recognise problems and tensions that can help inform future campaigning of this type.

Firstly, it is important to acknowledge that some members were confused by the 'Help a Child to Learn' campaign. At the time, education workers were exhausted, and many members could not see why union resources were being devoted to compensating for inadequate government funding. To some, it felt like the union was doing work the government should be doing, and therefore it was letting the government off the hook. This could not be further from the truth, as the union undertook basic solidarity work that was important for its own sake (as an act of class solidarity), but which also served to expose the inadequacy of government responses. However, this response does highlight the need to develop broader political work in the union, so the union's political campaigns are increasingly instigated and driven by members.

Secondly, we would highlight the difficulty in the national union trying to 'scale up' local grassroots campaigns, such as the work undertaken in Croydon and other branches, across the union. The desire to 'scale up' – and given circumstances, to do so 'at pace' – was understandable, but despite the national union trying to facilitate discussion and shared practice between all branches undertaking anti-poverty work and those interested in this work, these efforts ran aground. It may be that the national activity served to stifle, rather than develop, local initiative, and that more attention needs to be devoted to how local leaders can build from examples like Croydon horizontally at the base. Certainly, attention needs to be devoted to learning from the experience, with a focus on how national and local initiatives can connect in ways that preserve the energy of grassroots organisation.

One example of this grassroots activity, which began before the pandemic but developed in distinctive ways during the pandemic, was a meeting in April 2020 organised by a grassroots group called Celebrating Education. It was held on Zoom, and was attended by 2,000 educators. The meeting focused on rebuilding a broad and balanced curriculum in a post-pandemic world, and building alternatives to the existing broken assessment system. A follow-up meeting in June 2020 by the same group launched a 'Call for Evidence' that invited educators to submit their critiques of the current system alongside suggestions for alternative approaches. The Call attracted over 3,000 responses and acted as an important example of grassroots organising around alternatives. The meeting itself built off a major initiative the previous year in which union activists organised a conference at the Institute of Education in London attended by more than 500 participants. The event secured significant official support from the national union, but it was always activist-organised and managed. It also drew speakers and an audience from far beyond the union's activist base. One teacher blogged afterwards on the role the union was playing in shaping the narrative:

> I hope very much that the union builds on this successful day and takes 'Celebrating Education' to different parts of the country. If they can use their local networks to … get more people involved in the big education conversations, we can really scale up the proportion of our colleagues who are engaged in professional discourse. And the more are involved in the discourse the stronger we will collectively become. And god knows that we need to become stronger as a profession.[19]

By 2022, the impact of COVID on schools was much diminished, although transmission rates remained an issue, with all the implications for at-risk workers and students. What we have outlined here is the way in which the dramatic experience of the pandemic completely reshaped the terrain on which union activists were organising. For the NEU, it created the conditions in which its industrial and political strategies coalesced and forged a powerful bloc in both the workplace and in political and civil society. It also demonstrated how addressing the immediate concerns of members (literally whether going to work was safe or not) also provided a space to pose bigger and more fundamental questions about how the wider education system might be transformed. The prevailing 'common sense', often accepted only begrudgingly, was increasingly and openly challenged. Moments of crisis are moments of opportunity. However, whether such opportunities are realised depends ultimately on the decisions and actions of union activists as they navigate future struggles in new contexts.

CONNECTING INDUSTRIAL AND POLITICAL STRUGGLES BEYOND THE PANDEMIC: IS LEADERSHIP THE MISSING LINK?

Trade union activity is always experienced as a form of ebb and flow, when circumstances change and members are either drawn into activity, or they step away from such activity. The period of the pandemic was an obvious moment when a huge upsurge in NEU member engagement and activity was experienced and when the union's industrial and political strategies coalesced. But how can this activity be sustained in very different circumstances, sometimes when the immediate crisis appears to have passed and the situation appears more stable – or indeed, as the initial crisis develops into another, quite different, crisis? How can activists learn from moments such as the pandemic and continue to build union power?

The answer to these questions lies in understanding the role and importance of leadership in trade union organisations. By 'leadership', we are not referring to specific individuals, and we are definitely not referring to specific roles and positions in the organisation, but rather our interest lies in all those, at whatever level of the organisation and whether in formal positions or not, who perform the *function* of leadership. Leaders in trade unions are leaders by virtue of what they do, rather than who they are. This is not a leadership that is judged by the number of committees chaired, or that confuses 'busyness' with activism (both of which can be features of weak union organisation), but it is a leadership judged solely on its contribution to building the collective power of workers. It is leadership that recognises organising as an integration of practical and intellectual work[20] that connects immediate struggles with a political understanding of why change is necessary and how it can be secured.

During the period of the pandemic, the type of leadership we are describing emerged on a scale unprecedented in recent times, and was key to securing the victories, and government U-turns, that are outlined above. The linking of industrial and political struggle together challenged the government and employers on all fronts, at a workplace, local and national level. The national-level political campaign drew wide support from allies within and outside the labour movement and posed a serious challenge to the government's public narrative. At the same time, it was the organising at workplace level around collective letters, and later checklists, that made the campaign a reality on the ground. Throughout, the locus of power and control remained with the school or college groups, who had effectively established forms of informal collective bargaining at a workplace level, backed up by a national political position that provided strength and solidarity.

We have identified three dimensions of leadership that can help elaborate and explain effective leadership practices exhibited during the period of the pandemic: *strategic, critical* and *educative* leadership.

Our notion of *strategic leadership* draws on the work of Marshall Ganz (2009, 2010), and refers to the ability to develop a range of effective strategies through reading context effectively, mobilising resources, building and sustaining alliances, and making effective decisions based on sound analysis/assessment (Stevenson, 2016; Tattersall 2010). Throughout the pandemic, this aspect of leadership was evident at multiple levels, from national leaders who made effective judgements in response to government to local and workplace leaders who made these policy decisions real on the ground while also responding to local challenges and initiating collective action around these.

For example, in March 2020, when the country first went into lockdown, leaders in the union had to make a number of significant strategic calls, at national, local and workplace level.

Several months after the initial call for partial closure in March 2020, Kevin Courtney, joint general secretary of the NEU, described this first victory as 'a bit like riding the crest of a wave of public opinion'.[21] This was not a flippant remark about being in the right place at the right time, but rather an acknowledgement of the importance of assessing context and the collective strength of members in developing consciousness and framing collective action.

A few days before the union advised a significant group of members to work from home, such a move would have been unthinkable. It was only by responding flexibly to a fast-changing situation and making effective strategic decisions that the union was able to turn the context to its advantage. Both this initial decision and similar decisions throughout the pandemic, including in the run-up to June 2020 and January 2021, involved discussion and decision-making in an ongoing way at multiple levels to enable an effective response to the changing context.

However, while national leaders had to make the hard call to close schools and colleges in defiance of government advice, local and workplace leaders had to implement this decision on the ground, assessing the strength and confidence of workplace groups, negotiating with management, drawing up rotas, and enforcing (while sometimes also creating) union health and safety guidance. Strategic leadership was no less significant at the workplace level than it was nationally. As argued previously, the workplace became the key frontier of control during the pandemic, and workplace leaders had to constantly assess the balance of forces and the confidence of their members, then take strategic decisions with hugely significant consequences. In the best examples, these decisions were taken collectively and contributed to building the collective strength of the workplace group. This description of the approach to Section 44 action by a workplace rep was not untypical:

> We said, as a union group, we either all do it or we all don't do it. If one person objects, we need to know why and we will work around it. Perhaps those people who weren't sure felt buoyed by the rest of us because we were all going to back each other.

Building this level of workplace organisation, embedded by definition at the point where members face directly the frontier of control, provided the union with a vast reservoir of what Ganz refers to as 'salient knowledge' – detailed understanding of the key issues experienced by members in order to provide the best intelligence on which to develop strategy. In a trade union, this works most effectively when the union is integrally embedded within the workplace, not only providing salient knowledge of the key issues, but also ensuring strong motivation of leaders and robust reflective practices, including formal and informal accountability flows (see Ganz, 2009, 2010). At its most robust, this experience also exemplified Fairbrother's (1996) argument for the integration of representation and mobilisation, outlined in Chapter 2, as reps combined representation on issues of health and safety and more widely with collective mobilisation to address those issues. A collective culture was developed in many workplaces where members did not look to union representation from outside their workplace to solve problems for them, but organised collectively to solve them together.

Integral to all these developments were informal accountability flows, which brought the union leadership much closer to members in the classroom than would otherwise be the case. Arguably critical among these was the role of NEU Left, which hosted regular open meetings of grassroots members throughout the pandemic and fed back their views via the significant proportion of national and local leaders who were allied with NEU Left.

This regular source of grassroots initiative and feedback on developing strategy (including, for example, the initial idea of workplace letters in the run-up to June 2020 and the push to action in January 2021) acted both as a source of salient information and as an unofficial accountability flow which ensured that the voices of classroom educators were heard loud and clear at all levels of leadership in the union.

The second aspect of leadership we identified was *critical leadership*. Stevenson and colleagues talk about the importance of unions organising around ideas, which they define as 'taking seriously the need to reframe dominant narratives so that the values and aspirations of … trade unions are able to emerge as the common sense solutions to the challenges and crises that confront [us]' (2020, p. 39). By 'critical leadership', we are referring to all the ways in which representatives of the union engaged with members in a process of 'common sense disruption': challenging the normalised ideas and practices of the *status quo*, and working with others to articulate and popularise alternatives. Again, this is leadership that is only effective when it is exercised at every level of the organisation. At a national level, this chapter has highlighted some of the campaign initiatives the union promoted that challenged the logic of government education policy in the pandemic, but also used the moment to pose more fundamental and long-term questions about education funding, accountability models and wider questions of child poverty.

In defining critical leadership in these terms, we identify three constituent parts of that critical leadership. The first is the ability to identify, articulate and explain the challenges and contradictions workers experience in their work – to work with immediate struggles and to help workers to articulate these in ways that, literally, 'make sense' of their experience. The second is the ability to frame and articulate alternatives to the prevailing *status quo*. This goes beyond critique to connect with the possibility of an alternative. It rejects the notion that 'there is no alternative' by providing a language of hope and possibility. Finally, and crucially, it requires the capacity to cohere the collective sense of critique and possibility in ways that develop collective actions which challenge and resist.

Crucial to this aspect of leadership is the ability to form connections between sometimes quite abstract ideas and members' daily lived experience (Stevenson et al., 2020). This was most effective when workplace reps were able to situate the immediate issues faced by educators, from lack of adequate ventilation and excessive class sizes to overwhelming workload demands while teaching online and in person, in a broader context. These immediate issues were linked to a narrative around the crisis in public education – school cuts, rising class sizes, and the role of Ofsted and high-stakes accountability mechanisms as drivers of workload. At its best, workplace reps were able to directly link these developments to the impact of neoliberalism in education and to the impact of racism and sexism in the curriculum and within the system more broadly. This was possible in part because reps had undergone a common training that raised these ideological questions and situated the role of the workplace rep in the context of fighting neoliberal education reform. The same analysis was promoted in other training courses (including those for young members and local officers, and also targeted leadership development courses for women in leadership) and in union publications and speeches by national union leaders. When training was developed during the pandemic, this political analysis was then easily integrated into this new training for reps. One workplace leader, recruited as a COVID rep in summer 2020, described their experience of union training:

> One thing I thought was really good [about the training] was that it went beyond just the workplace and talked about things like solidarity and class struggle. I expected it to be more about the rights and responsibilities, but I thought that it was really good that it gave you more of a background. What does it mean to be in a union? What is solidarity?
>
> Our rights aren't something that's just given …. They're something that is hard won and fought for …. We're waiting for someone to come and do stuff for us. But we need to understand that actually, when we fight, we win. Can we build that into wider society, like the [Help a

Child to Learn] campaign? What do people want? What do they need? How can we fill that gap for them? If a union can do that, it can go beyond [the workplace] and become part of the community.

Critical leadership has to inform every aspect of union organisation, including leadership development among under-represented and oppressed groups. All those who act as leaders in the union, at whatever level, have a role in shifting the thinking and understanding of others. This must include not only members, but also other education workers, parents and the wider community. It is a process of developing and deepening consciousness (including our understanding of oppression and super-exploitation) that must inform every aspect of union work.

The third element of leadership we identified was *educative leadership*. By this, we are referring to the myriad ways in which leaders engage in the process of developing leadership capacities in others, individually and collectively. In drawing the distinction between organising, mobilising and lone wolf strategies to effect change, Hahrie Han (2014, p. 10) argues that:

The organiser makes two [strategic] choices: 1) to engage others, and 2) to invest in their development. The mobiliser only makes the first choice. And the lone wolf makes neither.

Educative leadership is the quality that makes the organiser different in Han's example. It is about investing in building leadership among others. It also involves building what Rick Fantasia (1988) refers to as 'cultures of solidarity' in workplaces, which strengthen the collective capacity of groups of workers. In the past, these cultures of solidarity were typically stronger. We are not indulging in 'golden age-ism' here, but recognising that, for example, the conditions that prevailed in the 1980s teachers' industrial action look very different today. Commitments to trade unionism were typically more robust, and expectations of loyalty to union decisions were often stronger. It is no surprise that this looks different today, because so much of what we have described in this book has been intended to disrupt these cultures of solidarity. The academies programme in English schools is not a technical reform to 'improve' education, but a class-based strategy to defeat organised education workers. This is the war on teachers.

Rebuilding these collective cultures in new and changed circumstances is now an urgent priority, and one that is intricately tied up with the question of leadership. As discussed in Chapter 4, workplace leaders play a key role in bringing together members in the workplace to act collectively. As such, they are a cornerstone of building a collective culture in the workplace. At the same time, this is a reciprocal process, and workplace leaders become the reflection of that collective culture in the workplace. A strong collective culture provides the conditions from which leaders develop, and will ensure continuity of leadership, in spite of membership churn and staff turnover.

However, building the kind of collective cultures we are describing involves a different type of leadership. The model of the expert local leader who appears (often from outside the workplace), solves problems for people, then disappears does nothing to build consciousness or collective culture. It is only through workers engaging in struggle and seeing in practice the power of collective action that consciousness, and collective culture, can develop. This requires leaders who see their key role as bringing others together to act collectively, to give them the power to solve the problems they face, rather than solving them on their behalf.

In the words of one workplace rep who had experienced this style of leadership:

> They don't swoop in and solve. They swoop in and enable us to do it. They're there for those people who aren't quite sure, but they give *us* advice and encourage *us* to do it. It's not a case of, 'We'll come into school and fix that for you.' It's always, 'You organise, you call a members' meeting. We'll support you to do it, but you do it, because you're the union.'

This aspect of leadership, which involves working alongside others to develop their skills, expertise, consciousness and power, we termed *educative leadership* because of the way in which it mirrors the approach to education outlined by pedagogical theorist Lev Vygotsky. Vygotsky (1978) posited that the most effective approach to education involves identifying what he termed 'the zone of proximal development' (p. 84), as the space between what a child is able to do unaided and what they are able to do with the support of a 'more capable peer' or adult (p. 86). By working alongside the child in this area, and supporting or scaffolding their problem-solving, the child develops their knowledge, skills and understanding in a way that expands their independent ability (and shifts their zone of proximal development).

This is an approach to teaching and learning which also applies in adult education and which we believe is directly analogous to building union leadership. It rejects top-down 'hero leadership' (the teacher or union activist as expert), and replaces it with an approach to human development that is shared and co-constructed. It recognises, in the words of Kevin Courtney, that 'Exclusively top down leadership will not work. Leadership must now also be local, upward and outward.'[22] This educative element was illustrated by one local officer who made the following point:

I think a lot of it is like teaching. You can't get anything out of your kids until you've got that relationship .... I learned so much from my co-rep who'd been a rep for 20 years. I made so many mistakes and I had to rewrite emails with him. I had to talk through with him about union meetings. I had someone training me on the job for many years before I could go in alone.

I try to replicate that co rep who was there for me. Whenever we get new reps, we always try to be that big sister, that big brother to them. It's very time consuming, but once you've built that relationship, they trust you, they know you've got their back and they will carry on doing what they're doing because they've got that motivation. They just need that support.

Educative leadership is the conscious development of leadership capacity in others, and the development of cultures of solidarity among groups of union members. It explicitly rejects individualised models of 'leave it to me' leadership in which dependency cultures are created between hero leaders and a passive membership. In their place, it poses collaborative and democratic leadership, which are collective in form and that replace dependency with inter-dependency and solidarity.

However, in presenting the case for educative leadership, we accept that making such leadership a reality poses considerable challenges. Many union activists find themselves unable to break out of the relentless tsunami of individual casework that fills their inboxes and voicemails. They want to work in different ways to build union power, but feel unable to make the jump from where they are to where they want to be. The heavy weight of individual cases and 'union business' keeps pulling them back.

Our view is that the problem of developing collective union power cannot itself be individualised by focusing on what some local leaders do or do not do, but rather the answer to developing the type of leadership described in this chapter requires a transformation of the union as a democratic space.

BUILDING LEADERSHIP IN THE DEMOCRATIC UNION

In our analysis of the pandemic, the NEU's national leadership exercised a significant and important role. The crisis in schools was developing rapidly, and urgent and decisive action was essential. We have also highlighted the vital role of leadership at the workplace level, as workplace representatives organised in schools to push back against the government's drive to open schools fully despite scientific advice to be more cautious. In many ways, the level of union leadership that is conspicuous by its absence in this analysis is that of the union branch. This is ironic because in the NEU, this is the basic democratic unit of the union, and it is also the layer of the union where most activist activity is focused. However, during the dramatic period of the pandemic, branches appeared to have a limited role. While many branch activists played a key role in supporting work in schools, the role of the branch itself was less clear. In many ways, this was reflected in the direct communications that opened up between the national union and workplace reps, and sometimes directly to individual members. While this communication was essential, it did not go unnoticed that there was a danger of branches becoming marginalised in a wider process of centralisation.

Our argument is that the experience of the pandemic simply made more visible a problem that has existed in the NEU for some time, and that is a direct result of the neoliberal restructuring of state education in England. Put simply, the union's branch structure has struggled to adapt to the new and much-changed environment of the English school system. Branch organisation is always complex in environments where branches include a large number of relatively small and geographically scattered workplaces. However, these problems are now exacerbated by a system of hyper-fragmentation in which several schools in close geographical proximity may all have different employers (or conversely, schools with the same employer are geographically dispersed). This is the consequence of academisation, and is a sharp contrast to the time when local NUT organisation was closely tied to the local authority system and therefore aligned with the local employer. The result can be a branch structure that feels 'hollowed out' and in which officer positions are not contested, conference delegates are seldom elected and branch meetings struggle for quoracy. This is by no means the situation everywhere, but it is a position too common for any activist to be comfortable with.

The process of union renewal we are describing remains a period of transition between an old that is dying and a new that is not yet born. In practical terms, it is illustrated by the account of one activist: Rina.

Rina's Story

In 2013, the government introduced performance-related pay for teachers. The NUT responded with a national campaign on appraisal and by asking workplace groups to refuse to comply with any appraisal policy which did not conform to the union checklist and to escalate to strike action. Rina was workplace rep at a secondary school where there were a number of ongoing battles between the school union group and the headteacher. One of these was over the appraisal policy.

Taking up the union's national campaign, Rina brought together her school union group and prepared them to escalate to strike action. When she had got them to the point where she felt they were ready to ballot, she put in a strike request. She was surprised when the branch secretary responded by refusing to process the request for a ballot and encouraging her to sit down and try to reach a compromise with the headteacher.

The branch secretary at the time, she argued, saw his role as to 'go in, listen to the grievances of the headteacher and try to sort out a deal'. As a result, there were a large number of settlement agreements, and the branch secretary was seen as a sort of 'mediator' between management and the membership.

'I think it was a complete and utter lack of confidence,' Rina said, 'that you couldn't actually challenge anything. Heads were very powerful, and your role was to be a part of that hierarchical structure and to facilitate the removal of "problem workers".'

'He couldn't have done anything else, as there was no sense of a workers' group, campaigning, organising. It was this one individual who came in to fulfil the requirement for a trade union official to be present .... It's worse than anything your enemies could do to you because it's someone on your own side saying you are powerless; you cannot fight this.'

Rina, who is now secretary of the branch, says she learned a lot from this experience about the impact a local officer can have on members' confidence. 'As far as I'm concerned, every single interaction with a member has to leave them feeling empowered .... I want to always let them know that it is possible to do something about it.'

This position in Rina's branch was not the result of the approach of one individual. It was a product of, and contributed to, a weakness in the local structures as a whole. While there were good workplace reps in some schools, they were isolated, carrying on their work in their own workplace. The local committee was dominated by retired members and a handful of 'proper stalwarts' who attended out of a sense of duty to the union.

Rina said she only went to the meetings out of a sense of loyalty to her co-rep, and described them as 'dull, dry and procedural. You would come away with nothing. I didn't know any better, but it certainly didn't leave me invigorated. There was very little connection with what was happening nationally, with what the national union was asking us to do.'

Rina got her strike ballot in the end, and her appraisal campaign was ultimately successful. This led to the local authority adopting a new policy across all of its schools. Rina argues that this was because they were concerned that what happened at her school might spread to others in the area. Eventually, Rina was encouraged to stand for election as branch secretary, and the branch looks very different now.

Rina's experience illustrates the type of 'intermediate leadership' that is crucial to union renewal. It rejects the 'leave it to me' model of leadership that was positively encouraged in the frequently paternalistic local authority system, and instead focuses relentlessly on building leadership in others, individually and collectively, at the workplace level. This type of intermediate-level leadership is crucial because in a hyper-fragmented school system, workplace organisation and leadership will always be too dispersed to automatically replenish itself. Building workplace organisation will always be ongoing work, and it is intermediate-level leaders who possess the salient knowledge to undertake this work. Leaders who work in this way know their workplaces, their members and those who have the potential to be developed as workplace leaders. They are uniquely placed to build the workplace organisation we described in Chapter 4, and where this intermediate leadership is widely dispersed (that is, undertaken by a broad network of activists), its potential for union-building in workplaces is amplified.

The type of leadership we are describing is crucial for union-building at the workplace, but it cannot be uni-directional, running from the branch to the workplace, but rather the relationship must flow both ways. Our argument is that the key to the revitalisation of branch democracy (and hence union democracy) depends on strengthening the link between workplaces and branches in ways that equalise this relationship. Too often, branches pass motions to send to annual conference that the vast majority members have not seen, let alone discussed. It is too easy for this to become an exclusive process driven by small numbers of activists – not intentionally, but inevitably, when branch organisation is weak. Our argument is that branch business needs to be driven by members in schools who meet, debate the issues important to them, and feed these into the branch. Creating an environment in which every workplace has a rep, and every rep is expected to attend branch meetings, is one basic way of consolidating this relationship. Formal power may reside in the branch (as the basic democratic unit of the union), but real power resides in the workplace, and strengthening this organic link between branch and workplace must be the imperative. This is only possible when intermediate-level leaders at branch level and workplace representatives in schools forge a genuinely organic relationship.

Here, we have argued that intermediate-level leadership provides the lynchpin role in building workplace organisation and in connecting members in the workplace to the national union. When this works well, there exists a strong accountability between 'the union' and members in schools. However, the role of intermediate leadership must not be restricted to these 'vertical' relationships, but leadership at this level must work horizontally too, connecting activists across branches. It is uniquely placed to do so. We believe that union democracy is strengthened when networks of grassroots activists combine together and organise. This may be activity that is organised by factional groupings, or it may be organised by looser self-organised networks. Such activity can deepen union democracy by contributing to a rich and vibrant union culture. However, what is vital is that such activities supplement, and do not substitute for, branch activity and democracy.

In presenting this analysis, we recognise that some of the arguments will be controversial. These are difficult problems (that extend far beyond the NEU), but they are also issues that require serious attention. There can be no union renewal that does not involve democratic renewal, and we hope that this analysis can help inform the open debate about these issues we think is necessary.

In summary, the experience of the pandemic disrupted every aspect of all our lives in ways that were unimaginable to most of us before anyone had heard of COVID-19. For the NEU, it was a moment when members demanded, and organised for, a collective union response to a seriously dangerous health and safety risk at work. The union's response was able to draw on its commitments to workplace organising and political campaigning in a way that delivered arguably the most effective union action of the whole period of the pandemic. It was the experience of the pandemic that created the conditions in which the union's industrial and political strategies, at local and national levels coalesced.

COVID created the context – but what brought the industrial and political campaigns together, and indeed what made that collective action effective, was the role of leadership, by which we mean leadership *by* the union (acting as a collective agent), and leadership *in* the union (exercised by individuals at every level of the union). There can be no understanding these developments without recognising the critical importance of leadership.

Our interest in 'leadership' is not in ways traditionally conceived in trade union organisations – the general secretary or the national executive committee. Nor is it only to be found in the union's rule book, being exercised at branch meetings and in committees. These are clearly important roles and structures, but our interest is in all those in the union who perform the *function* of leadership – acting as organisers in both a physical and intellectual sense (organising in workplaces and around ideas). These are the individuals in the union who deconstruct the common sense, inspire others around alternative possibilities and build the collective action that is the basis of any meaningful change. In this chapter, we have conceptualised this leadership as strategic, critical and educative. It is not leadership 'from above' or 'from below', but it is leadership exercised at every level of the organisation, and it transcends formal and informal structures. At its most effective, it is leadership that connects workplaces with the wider union organisation and which forges an organic unity across and through the organisation. It is a form of leadership that is crucial to building union power in any trade union context, and in the next chapter we outline how such leadership might be built across the labour movement.

7

Lessons in Organising

In a capitalist system, the conflict between classes is ever present. The visibility of this antagonism will inevitably ebb and flow. At times, it will be intense and highly visible, as organised workers push back against the efforts of employers to maximise the exploitation of labour. At other times, it will be less visible, with few obvious signs of worker resistance. What does not change, however, is the nature of the exploitation, as employers seek to maximise the value generated by their employees. Whether working in the private sector, where labour makes a direct contribution to profit, or in the public sector, where the nature of labour's contribution to generating surplus value is no less important, but is typically more indirect, the fundamental nature of the employment relationship is the same: one in which the employer seeks to maximise the surplus labour carried out by the worker. This is a relationship which in turn is defined by sex and race. Many members of the working class experience super-exploitation based on intersecting relationships of oppression.

In our analysis of this conflict between capital and labour, we have found it useful to draw on Antonio Gramsci's concepts of war of movement and war of position to help explain what we have presented as the war against teachers. Gramsci's war of movement emphasised the relationship between classes as one of direct confrontation (a 'frontal assault') in which the aim is to confront opponents in order to defeat and destroy. This is often visible in the actions of employers, but is also evident in the actions of the state as it mobilises its resources to challenge organised labour. In a UK context, this was presented starkly in the 1980s when the Thatcher government waged open war against the working class, recognising that defeating organised labour was key to ensuring that class resistance to exploitation could be demobilised. To this end, the state was able to deploy multiple strategies to engage in this war of movement – including a deliberately engineered recession (linked to deindustrialisation), privatisation, militarised policing, and the use of the law to curb both union power and the right to protest. All of this was consummately demonstrated during the miners' strike (a dispute the Tories used to inflict an immediate, but also symbolic, defeat on the working class). It was also evident in disputes with many others, including steel workers, printers, health care workers and, as we have shown here, teachers. It was a war waged on many fronts. It has also been ongoing, not least in the form of more and more legislation that aims to prevent or undermine strike action and criminalise acts of protest.

However, Gramsci's war of position identified a different type of struggle whereby a ruling group secured and maintained its dominance by winning broad support, or at least tacit acceptance, for the ideas that embedded its privileged status. In the decades since Thatcher came to power, the ruling class has engaged in a relentless ideological struggle to normalise the ideas and values that consolidate neoliberalism as the 'common sense' of the day. Individualism (and individual responsibility), traditional notions of the family, and conservative ideas about patriotism and nation ('Britishness', but often more accurately, 'Englishness') are all promoted as the norm, while solidarity (and collective action), deep democracy and radical social justice are all demonised. We are not suggesting that this is a simple process in which the working class are treated as stooges who uncritically accept the values and ideas of capitalism. On the contrary, we are arguing that this is a very complex process in which ideas seep into our collective consciousness, shaped by countless experiences every day that reinforce individualism and inequality as the natural order (Raymond Williams described this as a process of cultural 'saturation'; Williams, 1989, p. 74). Nor are we arguing that these ideas go uncontested and unchallenged. Rather, they are constantly disrupted in countless ways. What we are arguing is that we need to understand, and take seriously, the ideological struggle that has been waged against the working class. The struggle has not triumphed, but it has been effective at weakening collective culture, and now the labour movement and other organisations of the working class need to participate in the same struggle but be *more* effective than our opponents. In particular, we need to recognise and combat divisions based on race and sex, which have long permeated the labour movement, and understand how super-exploitation and oppression serve to maintain capitalism and the ruling class. In short, the labour movement needs to engage in its own war of position, alongside its readiness to engage in the war of movement that can erupt

any moment (indeed, engagement in a war of position is essential prepa-
ration for the war of movement). This requires the trade union movement
to build working-class power by acting industrially and politically, organising at the workplace, but also in political and civil society. Building this
type of trade unionism, industrially militant and politically campaigning,
is the strategic challenge facing the labour movement.

Earlier in this book, we framed this challenge as a choice between three
strategic options – the 'three Rs' of *rapprochement*, resistance and renewal.

Rapprochement reflects a tacit acceptance of the capitalist labour
market and the inequalities, injustice and denial of working-class power
that are the consequences of neoliberalism. It is based on the conviction
that employers and employees share common interests, and that where
there are conflicts of interest, these can be reconciled through a form
of social partnership. A feature of this approach is that it is fundamentally pessimistic about the ability and willingness of union members to
participate in collective action. The 'ordinary member' is often invoked,
and counterposed to 'activists', usually to justify inaction. Union power
is based on membership density (albeit a passive membership), a faith in
the ability of social dialogue to somehow deliver outcomes contrary to
the interests of employers, and the conviction that the power of a good
argument can persuade employers and governments to change course.

This strategy is a dead end. It is the approach that dominated trade
unionism in the UK for 40 years since the 1980s (and indeed, well before
that), and which has delivered little. It has no conception of how the collective power of union members must be mobilised to force employers or
the state to act against their interests.

The second strategic choice facing the labour movement is resistance, whereby union members take collective action (most commonly
strike action, but any form of industrial action) in order to operation-
alise their power, and force employers or the state to make concessions.
This is clearly important, and there is a key recognition that members
acting collectively is ultimately the source of union power. However, the
inherent danger is that members' willingness to take action is exagger-
ated. When this is the case, industrial action either fails to materialise
(in the UK context, because ballot thresholds are not met) or is poorly
supported, and is consequently ineffective. The result is often demoralised members, and internal recriminations and scapegoating (the union
'did not campaign hard enough' or made 'bad calls' about the type and

form of action). Members' reluctance to take action is rarely acknowl-edged, and there is no effort to seek to understand it. It follows that there is little effort devoted to shifting the thinking of those members who did not attend union meetings, did not vote in the ballots and who did not support the action. These are actually the union members who have a key role to play determining the success of any action, and whose thinking therefore needs to be shifted. Presented in more classically Marxist terms, they are the workers whose consciousness must be transformed. Engaging in struggle is crucial to any process of transformation, but in the absence of any spontaneous act of resistance, how can workers be brought together to act collectively?

Resistance, as we have described it here, is crucial, but on its own it is not enough. It fails to recognise workers as complex agents who hold diverse and often incoherent conceptions of the world. Its principal danger is that it assumes a homogeneity of worker interests, failing to recognise how divisions within the working class are maintained by cap-italism, and it can overestimate the readiness of workers to act in those interests. The result is poorly supported action which is likely to result in defeat. While it may be the case that defeats do not always demoral-ise, they often do. Members' perceptions that the union 'has no power' or 'strikes don't work' risk becoming self-fulfilling prophecies.

Our view is that a form of union renewal offers the only prospect of rebuilding union power because it recognises the need to work with members to actively build the types of campaigns (industrial and politi-cal) that can force employers and governments to retreat. It is a major step forward that this type of thinking is now widely understood in the trade union movement as debates about 'organising' and what it means have become increasingly common. We welcome the important and lively debates currently taking place that are necessary to chart ways forward that take account of the diverse contexts in which working-class struggles develop. In the sections that follow, we summarise our own contribution to these debates, based on the experiences set out in this book. Although we have grouped these ideas under three separate headings, they are interdependent and interlinked, and none of them can be considered sep-arately from any other. We offer these points not as external observers, but as labour movement activists, speaking about a movement of which we are part. Hence, within this text our references to 'we' are to ourselves as authors, but also as activists. We do not seek to speak *for* the movement, or *to* the movement, but from within, and as a part of, the movement. We hope our conclusions will have value for all engaged in trying to build an industrially militant and politically campaigning trade unionism across the labour movement. These three points are our 'lessons in organising'.

LESSON 1: THE UNION IS IN THE WORKPLACE

The purpose of trade unions is to build and exercise workers' power in (and potentially outside) the employment relationship. This involves engaging in a struggle over control of the labour process, based on what is an essentially antagonistic relationship between workers and employers. In the public and private sector, employer power is increasingly exercised by managers at the level of the workplace and it is certainly experienced by workers at the level of the workplace, therefore trade unions have no option but to contest it at the workplace. To do this, unions need to organise and build power at the workplace. This truth has not always been recognised historically, but it is ineluctable.

Therefore, any serious attempt at renewal must be driven by a relentless focus on workplace organising.

Fundamentally, there can be no workplace organising without workplace organisers. This is the key role of shop stewards or workplace representatives – to bring their co-workers together to act collectively. In Chapter 4, we explored the difference that union reps make to building collective action, at a workplace level and more widely. We called this the 'rep effect'. It is important to note that this is not simply about individual workplace leaders. Rather, workplace reps and strong workplace groups have a reciprocal effect on each other, forming a virtuous cycle of workplace organisation. In the strongest cases, the role of the 'workplace rep' is often carried out collectively by a team of reps.

Workplace reps perform three vital roles which build union organisation in and beyond the workplace.

First, they act as collective representatives of the workplace group, challenging management authority, presenting alternatives and supporting members to act collectively to win these alternatives. This relies crucially on the relationship they have with the union membership within the workplace (and sometimes the wider workforce beyond the union – there are many cases where effective workplace reps *de facto* speak on behalf of the entire workforce, regardless of union membership). In practice, this relationship, the key source of union strength, is far more important than the relationship reps have with management, which will be cultured to a great extent by the strength of their relationship with members.

The second key role of the workplace rep is to build a collective culture of organising in the workplace. This flows both from the relationships the rep builds within the union group and from the experience of acting and winning collectively. Workplace groups with a strong collective culture are those where there is an assumption that issues will be dealt with collectively and that members will listen to each other and abide by collective decisions. This does not necessarily mean regular, formal union meetings, because this is not how all union groups work, especially in smaller workplaces. It does mean an attitude of resolving things as a workplace group, collectively and without expecting solutions to come from outside.

This concept of collective culture has implications for union democracy. In much of our movement, branch democracy has been hollowed out. In many unions, branches cover multiple workplaces, employers or even industries, making it difficult to build a strong collective culture across the branch. Members' meetings often do not look like the 'leitmotif of union activity' described by Fairbrother (1996, p. 113).

The third key role of the workplace rep, therefore, is to build workplace democracy in the union and to act as the organic link to the formal democracy of the branch. This means that branches and branch meetings must be structured in such a way that the role of workplace reps is integral to their functioning. Having a clear focus within the agenda of meetings on reports and discussions of workplace issues, seeing national and regional campaigns as primarily delivered through workplace activity, and making sure workplace reps are central to branch decision-making are key.

In many cases, renewal may require the reorganisation of democratic structures to maximise the opportunity for member involvement in decision-making via their workplace reps. Such reorganisation must start from the principle of collective workplace organisation, and an organic link must be built between workplace leadership and branch. In some cases, such as geographically based branches covering several workplaces or industries, this will mean that branches must be reconfigured, either as smaller units based on workplace organisation or as a forum for the representatives of workplace collectives to come together and develop a common strategy for a common employer or industry. Either way, they should relate directly to the workplace collective. In doing so, it is possible to reconnect the formal democracy of the branch with the often informal, but in many senses more real, union democracy of the workplace, building leadership in the democratic union.

Clearly, building workplace reps is key to this entire strategy, in terms of rep density (most effectively measured by the percentage of members covered by a rep), but equally if not more importantly, rep effectiveness. By 'effectiveness', we mean reps with the confidence to exercise their role in the types of ways we are describing here.

In terms of rep development, unions must adopt targeted strategies for rep recruitment that focus not just on getting a name on a piece of paper or a number on a spreadsheet, but on building organised workplace groups, with a rep or reps as a key expression of this organisation. Issues-based organising, where organisers (whether union staff or lay activists) recruit reps as part of a process of tackling collective issues which have arisen in the workplace, is a fundamental part of this process. Going into any workplace with four key questions for collective discussion – What are the main issues in your workplace? What would a solution look like? Who is the key decision-maker? What are you willing to do to influence them? – is a great start. Workplace reps and organised workplace groups develop in the context of struggle. Identify the injustice. Attribute the injustice. Discuss the alternatives. Challenge the injustice, and win the alternative.

Once reps are recruited, training, supporting and mentoring them is key. Training must situate the role of the rep in the political, as well as industrial, context in which they will be organising, and must seek to develop their consciousness and leadership capacities, as well as their skills. This is explored further in the next two sections, but it is crucial that such training should be both formal and informal, with training provided by the union supplementing, not substituting for, activist-led training delivered in and through branches. All of this activity needs to be linked to mentoring from effective and experienced local leaders and the opportunity to network and discuss with other new workplace reps. New reps will learn most effectively through a process of practical experience with the opportunity for reflection. As with everything, a collective approach is key.

The fundamental building block in the contexts we have explored in this book is not the individual, but the organised collective. We must place these collectives at the centre of everything we do as trade union activists. We must turn the common conception of the union as a 'third-party' organisation (McAlevey, 2016) on its head (or, more correctly, stand it back on its feet). Organised collectives of workers, built from the workplace up, are the point of the union, and all other structures – national executives, regional offices, local districts, negotiators and officers – are auxiliary, and should be geared towards building and strengthening these collectives.

This is what we mean when we say the union is not in headquarters, it is in the workplace.

LESSON 2: ORGANISING MUST BE POLITICAL

Industrial struggle does not take place in a vacuum. As we saw in Chapter 2, the issues which workers face in the workplace have their roots in wider economic and political changes across society. Increasing precarity, the lack of workplace control and the downward pressure on wages and conditions which have become a daily experience for the majority of workers stem from political decisions made in Westminster, in 'free market' think tanks and in the boardrooms of global big business. These in turn have their origins in the economic shift to neoliberalism in the major capitalist economies. The scale of these changes is global.

This reality confronts workers when they struggle to change their working lives. On pay and job security, control of job content, on workload, there is a limit to what can be achieved at the level of the workplace. The wider economic and political context cannot simply be swept away solely by workplace struggle. Workers must wage a sustained political struggle in order to change the wider context. The decisions made in Westminster, from privatisation to austerity to the anti-union laws, affect workers' daily lives. Taking back control over our lives means engaging in political struggle.

It is important to note two things about this struggle.

First, political struggle is not synonymous with parliamentary politics, and it is definitely not something which can simply be 'contracted out' by unions to the Labour Party. What happens in Westminster, the influencing of political party manifestos and winning the support of MPs for legislative change are certainly part of politics, but they are by no means all of politics. For trade unions in particular, political action must be much broader. It involves developing mass collective action towards achieving political goals. It involves building broad-based community campaigns. It involves researching, targeting and pressuring corporations. It involves building mass support for political campaigns. It also involves politicising industrial action (for a further discussion of this, see Courtney and Little, 2014 or Little, 2016).

Under the UK's restrictive anti-union laws, industrial action to achieve political aims is illegal. Trade unions calling action on grounds deemed to be 'political' by the courts can have their assets seized and their officers prosecuted. However, even within this constraint, some unions have increasingly sought to politicise their action. This phenomenon is not limited to the UK, either. Similar laws to restrict collective bargaining to terms and conditions issues were introduced in Chicago, and yet, speaking about the 2012 Chicago teachers' strike, lead organiser Matt Luskin said:

> I don't think it is an overstatement to say that the overwhelming majority of [Chicago Teachers Union] members really believe that this was a strike against the neoliberal corporate reform agenda; really do believe that this was a strike about the future of education in Black and Brown neighbourhoods in particular, about the future of public education.[1]

Political action takes a variety of different forms, many of them extra-parliamentary. It is this extra-parliamentary political struggle which trade unions need to deepen and sharpen.

The second key point about political struggle is that it is not an alternative to industrial struggle. A number of trade union commentators and activists counterpose political struggle to building industrial power and focusing on the workplace. We absolutely reject this. The choice is not between Westminster and the workplace. The real question is how we build workers' power, from the workplace up, and at the same time politicise it, combining industrial and political struggle. Our aim should be to build our power to the point where workers begin to determine what happens in society, including decisions made in Westminster.

Capitalism divides the political and the industrial, allowing a limited, distorted and precarious form of democracy to exist in the former while excluding democracy almost entirely from the latter. It aims to restrict industrial struggle to purely economic matters of terms and conditions, limiting or banning entirely the right to strike on political grounds or in solidarity with other workers. Our aim should not be to perpetuate these divisions, but to break them down, embracing workers' struggle in all spheres. We must work to bring the mass power of our industrial strength into our political battles while seeking to politicise our industrial struggles.

At the same time as dividing the political and industrial power of the working class, capital fuses its own political and economic power together through the use of ideology – quite literally influencing the way people make sense of the world, and therefore how they act within it. Political and economic power are held together by ideology, which Gramsci argued acts like a kind of cement, binding and solidifying political and economic structures and securing the hegemonic leadership of the dominant class. It is in the field of ideology that the 'common sense' of society is established, the rules and boundaries of what can be said and thought, and all of the subtle influences that shape the way we view the world and inform the way we act. Ideology mediates how political and economic reality is experienced. Whether it is the crude tabloid stereotypes of greedy trade union 'barons' – and, as we have seen in our case, 'lazy teachers' – or the more subtle notion that inequality will always exist, ideology acts powerfully to shape the way we interpret the world, and therefore also our actions.

At the same time as linking political and economic struggle, therefore, unions must also act at the level of ideology to try to fracture the hegemony of the dominant class and open up further opportunities to fight and win. Part of this ideological work must be to develop the consciousness of our own union members through combining practical struggle with political discussion and reflection. This means that we, as a movement, must invest properly in political education, both formal and informal. This type of political education can provide a clear and coherent analysis of significant ongoing changes in the economy which allow union activists to understand how the issues they face are connected, to place themselves within the broader context, and to tailor their actions to contribute to a wider struggle over the future of society. Framed in this way, it can play a significant role in the developing consciousness of new reps and activists.

This deeper and broader approach to political education is an essential part of developing what McAlevey (2016) calls 'whole-worker organising'.

Workers are not one-dimensional. They do not cease to exist the moment they step out of the workplace. They are also parents, carers, service users, community members. Capitalism, and the multiple oppressions which are so entwined within it, impact on every aspect of their lives. From the underfunding and closure of hospitals to the privatisation of public transport, from the academisation of schools to benefit cuts and inflation rises, from endemic disability discrimination to the systematic racism and sexism faced by Black people and women, capitalism oppresses and exploits workers in and out of the workplace. If we really want to build collective power, we need to respond to the challenges faced by workers in every aspect of their lives. This means building the broad community alliances and political campaigns described earlier, but it also means challenging sexism, racism and all forms of discrimination, both within and outside the workplace. Commenting on US labour politics in his book *Class, Race and Marxism*, David Roediger notes that 'the "labor" struggle most able to sustain itself, that of the Chicago Teachers Union, has also been the one with the most sophisticated and energetic anti-white supremacist politics' (2017, p. 10).

The implications of this for the trade union movement are considerable. It is no longer acceptable (it never has been!) to dodge the question of the climate crisis and the ongoing problems of the 'fossil economy' (Malm, 2020) or to hold back from a position of opposition to war and militarism. We must build strong currents, within and outside our unions, fighting against racism and sexism, and against the discrimination faced by disabled and LGBT+ people. This is the only way we will connect our movement with the reality that workers face in their daily lives.

In the words of former UK Labour MP Laura Pidcock, we must:

> take our anger, take our pain, take our frustration, take our deep dissatisfaction with this system and occupy every single space with our politics, without embarrassment, without hesitation and without fear.[2]

Organising must be political.

LESSON 3: LEADERSHIP MATTERS

One of the most striking aspects of the NEU experience is that the union was successful when it was able to combine its industrial organising with political campaigning, fused together by ideological struggle which sought to break the neoliberal consensus. However, as we have highlighted, this has happened far too infrequently. Too often in the union's work there has been a disjuncture between industrial and political work which has meant that the workplace organising described in Chapter 4 was not sufficiently politicised and the political campaigning work described in Chapter 5 didn't fully harness the industrial power of the union and become real in the workplace.

The experience of the pandemic shows that this disjuncture can be overcome by that 'small but critical mass of activists' whose role involves promoting a sense of grievance by challenging accepted inequalities and creating or sustaining 'a high degree of group cohesion' (Kelly, 1998, p. 127) – in short, by the development of leadership. Particularly important is the work of intermediate leaders (between the workplace and the national leadership), whose role can be understood as a collapsing of the barriers between the political and industrial, and the national and local.

Our third lesson, therefore, is that leadership matters.

The fact that an increased focus on organising has, in some quarters, led to an increased focus on the importance of leaders is to be welcomed. Trade unions are increasingly taking seriously the importance of identifying and recruiting leaders into the union in order to build collective strength. However, it is time that we shift our focus, as a movement, from simply identifying and recruiting *leaders* to the more important question of how we build *leadership*. This focus on leadership is because, while recognising the critical importance of individual leaders, leadership in and of the working class must also be collective.

The reality is that without consciously and strategically building leadership within its own ranks, the trade union movement will wither inexorably. The concept of leadership set out in this book therefore draws on Gramsci's (1971) description of the leader as an 'organic intellectual' of the working class: a 'constructor, organiser, "permanent persuader"' (p. 10) who can connect the 'elementary passions of the people' to 'the laws of history (p. 418). This is an approach to building leadership within the class, not in response to some outside agency, but as a collective process arising from experience of working-class struggle and connecting that struggle to an understanding of the world. In Chapter 6, three aspects of leadership were identified – strategic, critical and educative – which are briefly recapped here.

Strategic leadership involves an ability to read the context effectively, to mobilise resources, build and sustain alliances, and to make effective decisions based on sound analysis/assessment. Drawing on the work of Marshal Ganz (2009, 2010), strategic leadership derives from the 'strategic capacity' of organisations and individuals. This, Ganz argues, rests on three elements – depth of motivation, breadth of salient knowledge and robustness of reflective practice. Clearly, from a trade union perspective, developing organic leaders from within the working class whose depth of motivation and breadth of salient knowledge depends on their ongoing connection to their class is a priority. The third element, robustness of reflective practice, draws us back to our first lesson, and the need to build and rebuild effective democratic structures and a collective culture within our unions, including developing an active left and rebuilding the crucial organic connection between branch leadership and workplace leadership.

Critical leadership comprises the ability to develop and sustain a critical understanding of the context in which trade unions operate, and to communicate this to others, inspiring them to action. By linking together a critical analysis of society as it is, an alternative vision of society as it could be and a belief in the power of collective action to change things, critical leadership inspires others to action and helps them construct a clear framework within which to act. Crucial to building critical leadership is the development of political education, both formally through the education and training structures of unions, and informally through reading groups, rank-and-file organisation and grassroots political discussion. This must be part of a wider shift across the movement in how we approach labour movement education, unshackling it from a functionalist focus on legal and representational skills and developing its transformative potential to build consciousness. Unions themselves must become sites of critical working-class political discussion and education, linking concrete experiences of collective action to a wider understanding of why and how society must be changed.

Educative leadership takes this pedagogical process one step further. It is about investing in building leadership among others, working with members as they collectively identify their own solutions and supporting new activists within those areas of leadership which they cannot carry out independently, but which they can with the support of a more experienced activist (paralleling the pedagogical approach of Lev Vygotsky, 1978). Key to this is giving workplace leaders and organised workplace groups the opportunity to solve their own problems through building their collective power, rather than swooping in and providing solutions from outside. As the old trade union maxim says: 'Never do for workers what workers can do for themselves.'

This approach involves building strong collectives, but also the use of one-to-one conversations to help developing leaders identify what assets they bring to the organisation, what barriers there are to their involvement and how they can overcome those barriers. It also means exploring their motivations for engaging in union activity and the contribution these make to the collective strategic direction of the union. These conversations provide the basis on which to give new activists responsibilities for leading on specific areas and tackling specific problems. This responsibility needs to include the space and flexibility to decide how to take on this leadership and approach these problems, but also the support and resources to deliver. The aim should always be to create opportunities to make, and learn from, mistakes, supported by and working alongside more experienced activists.

This work of leadership development needs to be specific, not generic, particularly when it comes to developing the leadership of underrepresented and oppressed groups. Women, Black members, disabled members and LGBT+ members not only face specific barriers to union involvement, but also bring assets and motivations that are specific both to their experience of oppression or discrimination and to them as individuals. The movement is weakened by these voices being marginalised and dismissed. Only through the development of clear pathways to leadership that engage and support these groups, building agency and power within the union, will the movement actually represent and draw on the strengths of the whole class. This should include formal leadership development for oppressed and underrepresented groups (for example, the NEU 'Women in Leadership' course), but must also be tied to an underlying culture shift and building informal leadership development opportunities.

Building leadership also requires us to restructure the way in which workplace groups and branches operate. They must become spaces for discussion and decision-making, not just the communication of information. Union members (in workplace meetings) and workplace reps (in branch meetings) must play a key role in this decision-making, leading meetings, not just participating in them. In many workplaces and branches, this will mean organising to change deep-set cultures that have built up over time. Workplace and branch meetings can also be used to collectively celebrate the work of newer activists, reinforcing successes, building confidence and making learning explicit. In this way, union activity can become a space for learning whereby those traditionally conceived of as 'leaders' increasingly hand over control and responsibility to others, building collective leadership in the process. This leads to significant change among the members of the collective. As Paolo Freire (1970) argued, in working together to change the world, the consciousness of the group is itself transformed.

Strategic, critical and educative leadership must be developed at all levels of the movement, but as argued earlier, the intermediate level of leadership (between the national and the workplace) is particularly important because of the role it can play in articulating the workplace and national, the industrial and political (see Figure 7.1).

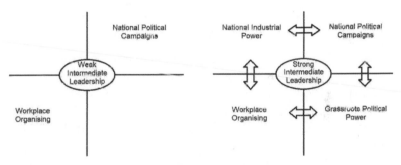

Figure 7.1   The importance of intermediate leadership

A weakness in this intermediate layer of leadership has serious consequences. Firstly, and pragmatically, there exists an inability to replenish national leadership or to develop grassroots leadership. Without intermediate leadership to sustain them, workplace structures can wither and die. Secondly, this weakness can cause a disconnect between the grassroots and national leadership, making it difficult, often impossible, to scale up grassroots (workplace) organising projects and to exercise industrial power beyond the workplace. Finally, because of the key role these leaders play in linking the industrial struggles of workers with political struggle, their absence can contribute to the divorce of these two aspects of building power, whose mutually reinforcing combination is necessary for renewal.

Rebuilding this intermediate layer of leadership must be an immediate priority right across the trade union movement. This must include looking at how the most engaged workplace reps and stewards and the most effective branch and regional leaders can begin to exercise that leadership collectively within the movement as a whole. By linking these leaders horizontally, on a cross-union basis, we can build the foundations of a strong reps/stewards/activists network that can exercise *strategic*, *critical* and *educative* leadership collectively at an intermediate level, right across the movement. Initiatives such as *StrikeMap*[3] represent steps in this direction and show some of what could be possible, but the development of a deeper, more embedded network of rank-and-file leadership across the movement is a priority which cannot wait.

As at other points in history (Murphy, 1934/1972; Seifert and Sibley, 2012), the organised left will have a key role to play in developing this layer of leadership across the movement, but it must be built on a broad basis, not a party or organisational basis. To be successful, this rank-and-file leadership network would also need to develop strong organic links, both to the wider layer of workplace leadership and to the national trade union leadership (in particular its left-progressive elements), strengthening and unifying the trade union movement around a critical anti-neoliberal political-industrial approach rooted in workplace organising and building workers' power.

Such cross-union co-ordination could be critical in terms of facilitating co-ordination of grassroots and national collective action in key industries and building a wider sense of working-class solidarity. Fletcher and Gapasin tell the story, in the preface to their book *Solidarity Divided* (2008), of a young progressive US union leader who, in an exchange with an affiliate of the Congress of South African Trade Unions made the observation that the role of a union is to represent the interests of its members. The reply from the South African trade unionists was diplomatic but clear:

> Comrades, the role of the union is to represent the interests of the working class. There are times when the interests of the working class conflict with the interests of the members of our respective unions.
>
> (Fletcher and Gapasin, 2008, p. ix)

The best way to strengthen this working-class solidarity is by building a cross-union co-ordination of leaders at multiple levels in the movement, something akin to the shop stewards movement that developed in engineering and shipbuilding at the end of the First World War or the movement built around the Liaison Committee for the Defence of Trade Unions in the 1960s and 1970s, but in ways that reflect the much-changed contexts that confront us today.

Building such a movement will not be easy. It will involve the broadest possible co-ordination of existing leadership at national, workplace and intermediate levels across the trade union movement. It will also rely on the involvement of the organised left, and crucially the active participation of that new layer of leadership being built in our unions now. But there is no alternative. The struggle to build a new national movement of shop stewards and activists is the new imperative.

FINAL WORDS

For at least half a century, the rich and powerful have been waging an open war against the working class, and in particular its most organised elements in the trade union movement. This is the continuation and latest intensification of a struggle that has been taking place since the development of capitalism as an economic system. The intention has not been to roll back the frontier of the state, as Margaret Thatcher once claimed, because the state's powers have been enhanced during this period. Rather, the aim has been to roll back the gains made by working-class organisation in the period when the welfare state was established. This was not a golden age for the working class, and in particular for women, Black, disabled and LGBT+ workers, whose oppressions and discrimination were, and still are, reinforced by the system. However, it was an age of advance and possibility, in which new struggles for social justice and democracy opened up paths to further progress. The growth of the women's liberation and civil rights movements, for example, highlighted the possibilities to work in and against the state, and to open up new prospects for progressive change.

It was precisely these possibilities that were so threatening to powerful and vested interests, and why these interests have mobilised on such a vast and sustained level to push back against all the achievements of the post-war era. The aim was to crush the 'Spirit of '45' and to defeat it, both industrially and ideologically. Industrially, the aim has been to weaken the trade union movement and prevent organised labour from securing a growing proportion of the national income for the working class. Ideologically, the aim has been to crush the ideas that promoted democratic control, social solidarity and an end to oppression as the foundational values of a progressive society – to establish the idea that there is no such thing as society as the everyday 'common sense' of our time.

Looking forward, it is not possible to predict the next stages in this struggle, nor the context in which it will take place. We may find ourselves in a period of protracted high inflation, in which the economic struggle between workers and capital will intensify as living standards drop. We may see increasing levels of wage militancy as workers fight back to maintain or increase their share of the national wealth. We may also see a chronic recession in which mass unemployment works to undermine the possibilities for collective action. What is certain is that we will see an increase in authoritarian rule, a trend already well established, with further legislation to restrict the right of workers to organise, to protest and to take collective action.

However, while we cannot predict the future, we can learn the lessons of the past and use them in rebuilding our movement to face whatever future awaits us. In the ongoing 'war of position', punctuated by moments of 'war of movement', where open attacks on trade unions and industrial action become commonplace, the health and strength of the movement must remain a long-term priority. Immediate struggles, whether defensive or offensive, must be seen in the context of building that long-term health and strength, to develop a trade unionism that is industrially militant and politically campaigning both in times of heightened struggle and the more difficult periods between.

It is in this context that we offer our 'lessons for organising', in the firm belief that *rapprochement* is a dead end, whatever the context, but that resistance alone is insufficient. Even in a period of increased industrial conflict and wins for the workers' movement, trade unions must set their course for renewal – changes in union form and organisation that focus forensically on actively building collective leadership, politicising and democratising the union – if we are to develop the capacity to win in the long run.

Renewal, in turn, must be built from the workplace up, rebuilding that collective culture in the workplace and linking this organically to formal democratic structures in our unions. Key to this is the role of workplace representatives in building strong workplace collectives, which form the basic building blocks of the union. This will mean structural and cultural change in many of our unions, to put workers' collective power at the centre of what we do every day, not just when we are on strike.

This power must be built politically as well as industrially. Political and industrial campaigns must be combined, along with a clear focus on directly engaging in ideological struggle – building consciousness by disrupting the accepted 'common sense'. Union action cannot be restricted to challenging the consequences of neoliberalism, but must also be focused on challenging the ideas, and the structures, that are the root cause of the problems workers face. This is one of the key conclusions to be drawn from the experience of the NEU and NUT that has been presented in this book. But this political campaigning does not mean focusing exclusively on parliamentary politics – or even worse, contracting this work out to the Labour Party. Rather, workers, through their unions, must engage in mass extra-parliamentary political struggle in order to win, and industrial and political struggles must be co-ordinated and connected at every level of the union, reaching right into the workplace. Unions cannot restrict themselves to narrow economistic struggles (important as they are), but must always link these to wider questions of democratic control, within and beyond the workplace. There can be no union renewal that is not fundamentally about democratic renewal – in the union, in the workplace and in society.

Crucial to all of this is building strategic, critical and educative leadership at every level in the movement. This will mean developing organic leaders from within the working class as part of rebuilding democratic structures and collective culture within our unions. It will mean a new approach to labour movement education which focuses on the political and ideological, recognising the transformative potential of education in struggle and the key role of the organised left within the movement. It will mean building truly educative leadership – leaders who see their role as supporting the development of leadership in others, as building power through agency and collective culture.

Most importantly, this leadership must be brought together across the movement to provide co-ordination and collective leadership from the grassroots up. The need for a new national movement of shop stewards and activists is one of the most pressing priorities for our movement today, and is the key to building workers' power and renewing our unions for the struggle ahead.

In presenting these 'lessons', we do so in the spirit of the collective learning that we believe is essential in our movement. Our contribution presented here is based on our experiences working in and with the NUT and NEU. We hope that there is much to be learned from our analysis, but inevitably whatever is useful will only be so if it is reframed and re-applied in the specific context of particular struggles. The process of renewal we have outlined is always a work in progress. It can never be complete and is always being formed and re-formed in struggle and through struggle. The NEU has achieved some significant victories, but we do not present this as an unqualified success story. There is still too much that needs to be done to claim success. Nor do we claim that our analysis is in any sense definitive. Rather, our 'lessons' are offered as a contribution that we hope will inform thinking and generate debate. There are no right answers, only ideas that are tested through struggle, and then adapted and reframed.

Notes

CHAPTER 1

1. *Daily Mail*, 9 December, 2012, 'Gove on "war footing" with teaching unions expected to launch industrial action over pay as he considers new anti-strike laws'. Available online at: www.dailymail.co.uk/news/article-2245459/Gove-war-footing-teaching-unions-expected-launch-industrial-action.html [accessed 5 September 2022].

2. National Foundation for Educational Research (NFER) (2013) *NFER Teacher Voice Omnibus November 2012 Survey: Understanding Union Membership and Activity*, London: DfE. Available online at: https://assets.publishing.service.gov.uk/government/uploads/system/uploads/attachment_data/file/219648/DFE-RR268.pdf [accessed 5 September 2022].

3. *Sunday Times*, 9 December, 2012, 'Gove's war over pay for teachers'. Available online at: www.thetimes.co.uk/article/goves-war-over-pay-for-teachers-6m8g5dvlrv2 [accessed 5 September 2022].

4. In NFER (2013), the results indicated that 97% of teachers were members of a trade union.

5. Department of Education and Science (1967) *Children and Their Primary Schools: A Report of the Central Advisory Council for Education (England), Volume 1: The Report*, London: HMSO.

6. The phrase 'exam factory' is borrowed from a report by Merryn Hutchings for the NUT titled *Exam Factories? The Impact of Accountability Measures on Children and Young People*. Available online at: www.basw.co.uk/system/files/resources/basw_112157-4_0.pdf [accessed 5 September 2022].

7. NEU press release, 2 January 2021, 'NEU Advises Primary Members It Is Unsafe to Return to Work'. Available online at: https://neu.org.uk/press-releases/neu-advises-primary-members-it-unsafe-return-work [accessed 5 September 2022].

8. *Schools Week*, 4 January, 2021, 'The back to school debacle: a week of blundering U-turns'. Available online at: https://schoolsweek.co.uk/the-back-to-school-debacle-a-week-of-blundering-u-turns/ [accessed 5 September 2022].

9. This book focuses on the NEU and NUT. The reason for this is discussed later in this chapter.

10. TUC (2022) *Still Rigged: Racism in the UK Labour Market*. Available online at: www.tuc.org.uk/research-analysis/reports/still-rigged-racism-uk-labour-market [accessed 5 September 2022].

11. See Office for National Statistics (2021) *Gender Pay Gap in the UK: 2021*. Available online at: www.ons.gov.uk/employmentandlabourmarket/peoplein work/earningsandworkinghours/bulletins/genderpaygapintheuk/2021 [accessed 5 September 2022].

12. See *Closing the Gender Pay Gap in Education*. Available online at: www.naht. org.uk/Our-Priorities/Our-policy-areas/Equality-diversity-and-inclusion/ ArtMID/824/ArticleID/1414/Closing-the-Gender-Pay-Gap-in-Education-A-leadership-imperative [accessed 5 September 2022].

13. See *The Guardian*, 25 January 2022, '"There is absolutely systemic racism": BAME headteachers share their views'. Available online at: www.theguardian. com/world/2022/jan/25/there-is-absolutely-systemic-racism-bame-headteachers-share-their-views [accessed 5 September 2022].

14. *It's Just Everywhere – Sexism in Schools*. Available online at: https://neu.org. uk/advice/its-just-everywhere-sexism-schools [accessed 5 September 2022].

15. See *The Guardian*, 24 March 2021, 'Exclusion rates five times higher for black Caribbean pupils in parts of England'. Available online at: www. theguardian.com/education/2021/mar/24/exclusion-rates-black-caribbean-pupils-england [accessed 5 September 2022].

16. See NEU, *Anti-Racism Charter*. Available online at: https://neu.org.uk/anti-racism-charter [accessed 5 September 2022].

17. See NEU, *Breaking the Mould*. Available online at: https://neu.org.uk/breaking-mould [accessed 5 September 2022].

18. Our analysis in this volume is not concerned with differences between these bodies, and any reference in the text can be taken to refer generically to a formal union group that exists immediately above the level of the individual workplace.

19. Due to these differences, this book focuses on the situation in England. While the NUT organised across England and Wales and the NEU organises across England, Wales and Northern Ireland, this does not mean we can simply read across from one education system to another.

20. In the UK, 'state education' refers to public sector education. It is the term used throughout the book, and is equivalent to 'public education' and 'public schools' in many other jurisdictions.

CHAPTER 2

1. TUC (2020) 'Trade union membership rises for third year running to 6.4 million'. Available online at: www.tuc.org.uk/blogs/union-membership-rises-third-year-running-64-million [accessed 5 September 2022].

2. This book was finalised in the autumn of 2022. At the time, inflation was over 10%, with some forecasts predicting a rise to nearer 20% in 2023. This was the main factor that was contributing to a potential 'autumn of discontent' with strikes across several industries. High inflation is unlikely to disappear quickly, and it is probable that this will further drive a new trade

union militancy. This increase in worker confidence is very welcome, but should not obscure the need for a hard-headed analysis of the challenges that will continue to confront the labour movement.

3. Office of National Statistics (2018) *Labour Disputes in the UK, 2018*. Available online at: www.ons.gov.uk/employmentandlabourmarket/peopleinwork/ workplacedisputesandworkingconditions/articles/labourdisputes/2018 [accessed 5 September 2022].

4. Goodrich's study of the 'frontier of control' took place in Britain in the early twentieth century. His interest was in workers' control of industry, and the concept of the frontier of control was developed to describe the line (rarely visible, and always contested) between managerial authority and worker control of the labour process.

5. Unofficial industrial action is action that takes place outside of established procedures for dealing with workplace disputes. It is heavily circumscribed by UK anti-trade union legislation.

6. 'Facilities time' refers to paid release time that a union officer may have to undertake union duties. It is usually provided through a negotiated agreement with the employer, and is employer-funded. It is intended to facilitate 'good industrial relations'. In the school sector, local union officers ('lay members/officers') are not paid for by the union.

7. The white paper, Department of Employment and Productivity (1969) *In Place of Strife: A Policy for Industrial Relations*, Cmnd 3888, London: HMSO, proposed that strikes could only take place after a ballot of members, and an Industrial Board was also proposed that could enforce settlements. Its publication provoked a major backlash from the trade union movement, and the proposals did not become law. However, many of the key ideas did re-emerge in Labour's Trade Union and Labour Relations Act 1974.

8. Arguably the most high-profile example was the case of the 'Pentonville Five'. These were five dock workers who were imprisoned for disregarding a court order to stop their picket in East London. Their imprisonment promoted large-scale strike action and the possibility of a general strike. Within a week of their imprisonment, the five were released, ostensibly on legal grounds, but almost certainly due to the huge campaign that had developed in their support.

9. Historically, the UK industrial relations system had been described as 'voluntarist' precisely because it was characterised by voluntary interactions between employers and trade unions. The state had very little direct intervention. This has changed dramatically and beyond recognition.

10. Under UK trade union legislation, official industrial action must be preceded by a ballot of all members involved. The ballot must be conducted by post, and the Conservative Party has resisted all efforts to allow electronic voting. In 2016, the law additionally required that disputes would only be legal if at least 50% of members voted, and in some key services at least 40% of the those balloted had to vote in favour of action. These are high thresholds

for postal ballots, and are higher than the election turnouts in many local council elections, for example.

11. See, for example, the GMB and Communication Workers Union's joint paper, Edmonds and Tuffin (1990).

12. 'Organizing for Power – Workers Rising Everywhere' was established in 2019, and describes itself as 'A skills-focused training and networking program for organizers worldwide'. It is hosted by the Rosa-Luxemburg-Stiftung, and is based around the organising model presented by Jane McAlevey and colleagues. Details are available at https://rosalux-geneva.org/events/organizing-for-power-workers-rising-everywhere/ [accessed 5 September 2022].

13. This was evident in the 2022 UK higher education disputes, when action involving relatively few members in a high-stakes and strategically impactful assessment and marking boycott achieved breakthroughs that protracted strike action by larger numbers of members had not.

14. See, for example, the experience of the 1970 Newark teacher strikes analysed in Golin (2002).

15. *The Schools Chicago Students Deserve: Research-based Proposals to Strengthen Elementary and Secondary Education in the Chicago Public Schools* was produced by the Chicago Teachers' Union. The original version is no longer available, but a Version 2.0 is available online at: www.ctulocal1.org/reports/schools-chicagos-students-deserve-2/ [accessed 5 September 2022].

16. Structure tests are activities that allow union activists to literally test the strength of organising structures in mobilising members. Structure tests can be high-profile (such as strike ballots), but can also be low-key and informal. The important issue is that they provide union organisers with a 'measure' of member organisation.

CHAPTER 3

1. *Spirit of '45* is a 2013 film directed by Ken Loach which traces the building of the post-war welfare state in the UK.

2. For a detailed account of education policy in post-war Britain, we recommend Jones (2016).

3. Department of Education and Science (1967) *Children and Their Primary Schools: A Report of the Central Advisory Council for Education (England), Volume 1: The Report*, London: HMSO.

4. For further discussion of the links between Hayek, Pinochet and the New Right across North America and the UK, see Harvey (2007).

5. As its name suggests, ALTARF existed to develop anti-fascist and anti-racist work in schools and in schools' communities. It produced a range of publications to support teachers in engaging in anti-racist education, including *Challenging Racism* (ALTARF, 1984).

6. For a presentation of the teachers' version of the events, see Ellis et al. (1976).

7. See, for example, the role of the Technical and Vocational Education Initiative (TVEI) in schools that was famously managed by the Manpower Services Commission (a non-departmental offshoot of the Department of Employment) rather than by the Department for Education and Science. The TVEI was technically not part of the National Curriculum, but it cannot be viewed as separate from it.

8. For those who want to get some sense of the vitriolic attack by the Thatcher government on teachers, the new metropolitan left within bodies such as the ILEA and oppressed groups such as the LGBT+ communities, Margaret Thatcher's speech to the 1987 Tory Party conference is an important, if difficult, listen. It is available online at: https://youtu.be/GrsA_-FbxTs [accessed 5 September 2022].

9. See *The Guardian*, 14 March 2014, 'Teachers: life inside the exam factory'. Available online at: www.theguardian.com/education/2014/mar/14/teachers-life-inside-the-exam-factory [accessed 5 September 2022].

10. Headteacher interview, February 1994, conducted for Stevenson (2001).

11. The workload agreement was finalised in 2003 – *Raising Standards and Tackling Workload: A National Agreement*. Available online at: https://dera. ioe.ac.uk/540/1/081210thenationalagreementen.pdf [accessed 5 September 2022].

12. For a comprehensive analysis of the period of Social Partnership, see Carter, Stevenson and Passy (2010).

13. DfE, *The Importance of Teaching: The Schools White Paper 2010*. Available online at: https://assets.publishing.service.gov.uk/government/uploads/system/uploads/attachment_data/file/175429/CM-7980.pdf [accessed 5 September 2022].

14. Interview with David Cameron, Conservative Party leader, in the *Daily Telegraph*, 9 February 2009. The text is available online at: https://conservativehome.blogs.com/torydiary/2009/02/cameron-vows-to.html [accessed 5 September 2022].

15. In November 2011, Tory-controlled Lincolnshire County Council announced that it wanted all its schools to become academies. See Channel 4 News, 24 November 2011, 'The "education revolution" sweeping Lincolnshire'. Available online at: www.channel4.com/news/the-education-revolution-sweeping-lincolnshire [accessed 5 September 2022].

16. In October 2020, Conservative Women and Equalities Minister Kemi Badenoch said in parliament that teachers who did not provide 'balance' when discussing white privilege were acting illegally. See *The Guardian*, 20 October 2020, 'Teaching white privilege as uncontested fact is illegal, minister says'. Available online at: www.theguardian.com/world/2020/oct/20/teaching-white-privilege-is-a-fact-breaks-the-law-minister-says [accessed 5 September 2022].

17. In March 2013, Michael Gove responded to a letter signed by 100 academics criticising government policy by describing them as 'the enemies of promise'

and acting like 'the Blob'. See *Daily Mail*, 23 March 2013, 'I refuse to surrender to the Marxist teachers hell-bent on destroying our schools': Education Secretary berates "the new enemies of promise" for opposing his plans'. Available online at: www.dailymail.co.uk/debate/article-2298146/I-refuse-surrender-Marxist-teachers-hell-bent-destroying-schools-Education-Secretary-berates-new-enemies-promise-opposing-plans.html [accessed 5 September 2022].

18. *Schools Week*, 26 May, 2022, '"By schools for schools": Institute of Teaching winners finally revealed'. Available online at: https://schoolsweek.co.uk/institute-of-teaching-winners-finally-revealed-dfe-education-teacher-training/ [accessed 5 September 2022].

19. From a speech Secretary of State Michael Gove delivered at the National College for Teaching and Leadership, 25 April 2013. Available online at: www.gov.uk/government/speeches/michael-gove-speech-to-teachers-and-headteachers-at-the-national-college-for-teaching-and-leadership [accessed 5 September 2022].

CHAPTER 4

1. From an interview conducted with an NUT rep who led a campaign against the academisation of her school. The campaign involved eight days of strike action. The research was published in Stevenson (2016).

2. The internal report, 'The Next Five Years: Implications for the Union: Consultation Paper', was produced in 1992, shortly after the Conservative Party won the general election and when it became apparent the 1988 reforms would not be reversed by a change of government.

3. From research conducted for the British Educational Leadership, Management and Administration Society-funded project *School Sector Industrial Relations in Transition* (2011–2012). Available online at: www.belmas.org.uk/write/MediaUploads/Stevenson_Mercer_Final_Report.pdf [accessed 5 September 2022].

4. From an interview conducted with a leading member of the Save Downhills campaign. The research was published in Stevenson (2016).

5. Interview conducted with NUT school rep, reported in ibid.

6. See *Organising to Win: How Nottingham Teachers Defeated the Five Term Year and Organised Their Union*. Available online at: https://vote4sheena.files.wordpress.com/2014/03/organisingtowin.pdf [accessed 5 September 2022].

7. Blower, C., *Morning Star*, 18 April 2015, 'Empowering lay structures'. Available online at: https://morningstaronline.co.uk/a-6e5a-empowering-lay-structures [accessed 5 September 2022].

8. These data were collected as part of an unpublished internal research project for the NUT carried out by Howard Stevenson and Emily Winchip at the University of Nottingham in 2017.

9. Ibid.

10. See NEU, *Annual Conference 2019 – Resolutions*. Available online at: https://neu.org.uk/sites/default/files/2019-05/Annual%20Conference%20 Resolutions%202019.pdf [accessed 5 September 2022].

11. The research project was carried out by Howard Stevenson and Emily Winchip at the University of Nottingham, but not published.

12. The methodology used Mokken scale analysis and Rasch analysis to construct the scale of member commitment and participation. Data design and analysis were carried out by Emily Winchip. A detailed discussion of the use of this type of scale analysis, used in another context, is set out in Winchip (2022).

13. In Figure 4.1, the distribution pattern is an approximate representation to help visualisation, although the peak points are accurately represented.

14. From Stevenson and Winchip's research in 2017.

15. All of the information provided in this example was provided by Branch Secretary Alex Kenny.

16. Personal communication with the authors.

17. In 2022, a government white paper, *Opportunity for All: Strong Schools with Great Teachers for Your Child*, committed to all schools being part of a Multi-Academy Trust within a 'Trust-led system'. Available online at: https://assets.publishing.service.gov.uk/government/uploads/system/uploads/attachment_data/file/1063602/Opportunity_for_all_strong_schools_with_great_teachers_for_your_child__print_version_.pdf [accessed 5 September 2022].

18. 'Possible Structures for Academy Chains'. NUT Executive Committee paper TGRM23/12, 6 September 2013 (internal document).

CHAPTER 5

1. Michael Gove's speech 'The Progressive Betrayal' to the Social Market Foundation, 5 February, 2013. Available online at: www.smf.co.uk/michael-gove-speaks-at-the-smf/ [accessed 5 September 2022].

2. 'The Blob' was a term used by Michael Gove to refer to the 'educational establishment' of 'progressive educators'. His attack on 'the Blob' was presented in an article in the *Daily Mail*, 23 March 2013, 'I refuse to surrender to the Marxist teachers hell bent on destroying our schools: Education Secretary berates "the new enemies of promise" for opposing his plans'. Available online at: www.dailymail.co.uk/debate/article-2298146/I-refuse-surrender-Marxist-teachers-hell-bent-destroying-schools-Education-Secretary-berates-new-enemies-promise-opposing-plans.html [accessed 5 September 2022].

3. The most obvious example is the American E. D. Hirsch, whose statement for a 'core knowledge curriculum' is set out in his book *The Schools We Need:*

And Why We Don't Have Them (1999). The book is dedicated to 'the Teachers and Principals of Core Knowledge Schools' and to Antonio Gramsci.

4. Teach meets emerged as a grassroots form of self-organised teacher professional development. Often organised using social media, teach meets provided a space for teachers to share their work with peers in an environment free from managerial agendas and judgements. Teach meets developed as a direct response to the growing managerial control of teachers' professional autonomy.

5. *Northern Rocks* was established as a teacher self-organised conference, held in Leeds, and with an ethos quite different to the type of events being organised by powerful groups with connections to right-wing politicians and think tanks. After a break (one of its main organisers, Emma Hardy, became a Labour MP in 2017), *Northern Rocks* was re-established in 2022.

6. GERM is an acronym for the Global Education Reform Movement. See Pasi Sahlberg, 'How GERM is Infecting Schools Around the World?' Available online at: https://pasisahlberg.com/text-test/_[accessed 5 September 2022].

7. See T. Dowling, 23 April 2014, 'NUT Conference Report: Engage, Pressure, Strike!' Available online at: www.counterfire.org/news/17179-nut-conference-report-engage-pressure-strike [accessed 5 September 2022].

8. 'Our Strategy for a Big Conversation', NUT internal document, 16 July 2014.

9. Ibid.

10. Michael Gove was sacked as Education Minister in July 2014. Lynton Crosby, the Conservative Party's Campaigns Director, argued that Gove was 'toxic' among teachers, and with an election imminent, Gove was dismissed. See *The Guardian*, 15 July 2014, 'David Cameron axes Michael Gove in reshuffle after toxic poll warning'. Available online at: www.theguardian.com/politics/2014/jul/15/cameron-sacks-toxic-gove-promotes-women-reshuffle [accessed 5 September 2022].

11. *The BETT Show* is, according to Wikipedia, 'a global series of education shows organised by Hyve Group marketing information technology in education. The flagship show is located in the UK, with satellite events in Asia & Brasil.' *Wikipedia*, 'BETT'. Available online at: https://en.wikipedia.org/wiki/BETT [accessed 5 September 2022]. Nicky Morgan's speech in 2015 is available online at: www.gov.uk/government/speeches/nicky-morgan-speaks-at-the-2015-bett-show [accessed 5 September 2022].

12. The government's white paper *Education Excellence Everywhere* (2016) claimed to set out the government's 'vision for schools in England'. Available online at: www.gov.uk/government/publications/educational-excellence-everywhere [accessed 5 September 2022].

13. *The Guardian*, 6 May 2016, 'Government drops plan to make all schools in England academies'. Available online at: www.theguardian.com/education/2016/may/06/government-backs-down-over-plan-to-make-all-schools-academies [accessed 5 September 2022].

14. Ibid.

15. The Labour Party's manifesto in 2017 was titled *For the Many Not the Few*. Available online at: https://labour.org.uk/wp-content/uploads/2017/10/labour-manifesto-2017.pdf [accessed 5 September 2022].
16. Discussed in *Schools Week*, 19 March 2018, 'NUT spent £326k on general election campaign'. Available online at: https://schoolsweek.co.uk/nut-spent-326k-on-general-election-campaign/ [accessed 5 September 2022].
17. See BBC Online, 26 May 2017, 'Is this the start of a return for the teaching unions?' Available online at: www.bbc.co.uk/news/education-40063060 [accessed 5 September 2022].
18. See *TES Magazine*, 14 June 2017, '750,000 voters switched support as a result of school funding cuts, survey finds'. Available online at: www.tes.com/magazine/archive/750000-voters-switched-support-result-school-funding-cuts-survey-finds [accessed 5 September 2022].
19. *It's Just Everywhere – Sexism in Schools*. Available online at: https://neu.org.uk/advice/its-just-everywhere-sexism-schools [accessed 5 September 2022].
20. Rules were also introduced to ensure that at least 50% of the new union's national executive were women – a demand long campaigned for by women activists in the NUT.
21. NEU internal document, 'NEU Mission Statement' (2017).
22. Ibid.

CHAPTER 6

1. Unless otherwise indicated, interview data presented in this chapter were collected in 2022 specifically for this publication.
2. Typically, training teachers were recruited into 'student membership' of the education unions at recruitment fairs organised by the unions in partnership with the teacher training colleges and universities. With the transition to 'school-based' routes into teaching, it has become more difficult for education unions to recruit training teachers before they become fully qualified.
3. Indicative ballots are unofficial ballots conducted by trade unions to test member commitment prior to proceeding to a full official ballot (required by law in the UK). Indicative ballots act as a 'structure test', ensuring that if the union proceeds to a full ballot, there is a strong chance of securing a 'yes' vote and meeting the threshold requirements for the ballot to be legally valid.
4. See *Huffington Post*, 30 August 2020, 'Exclusive: teachers' union added 50,000 members in Covid pandemic'. Available online at: www.huffingtonpost.co.uk/entry/50000-rise-in-neu-teachers-union_uk_5f496bf4c5b64f17e13d9401 [accessed 5 September 2022].
5. See *Daily Telegraph*, 7 February 2021, 'Teachers "using Covid pandemic to push for pay rise"'. Available online at: www.telegraph.co.uk/news/2021/02/07/teachers-using-pandemic-push-pay-rise/ [accessed 5 September 2022].
6. Letter to Boris Johnson, 17 March 2020. Available online at: https://neu.org.uk/media/9531/view [accessed 5 September 2022].

7. Independent SAGE was established as an alternative to the government's official body established to provide expert advice on the pandemic. Questions were raised about the political independence of the government-appointed body, so an independent alternative was established by a group of prominent and esteemed experts. Their reports, including those related to the education sector, can be accessed at www.independentsage.org/.

8. See *The Guardian*, 19 March 2020, 'Boris Johnson: UK can turn tide of coronavirus in 12 weeks'. Available online at: www.theguardian.com/world/2020/mar/19/boris-johnson-uk-can-turn-tide-of-coronavirus-in-12-weeks [accessed 5 September 2022].

9. *NEU Left Bulletin*, December 2020.

10. See NEU, 31 December 2020, 'On 22 December SAGE told government to close schools', press release. Available online at: https://neu.org.uk/press-releases/sage-told-govt-close-schools [accessed 5 September 2022].

11. See 'Prime Minister's address to the nation: 4 January 2021'. Available online at: www.gov.uk/government/speeches/prime-ministers-address-to-the-nation-4-january-2021 [accessed 5 September 2022].

12. See NEU, 11 June 2020, 'Coronavirus: National Education Recovery Plan', press release. Available online at: https://neu.org.uk/press-releases/coronavirus-national-education-recovery-plan [accessed 5 September 2022].

13. See *NEU Education Recovery Plan*. Available online at: https://neu.org.uk/media/14241/view [accessed 5 September 2022].

14. NEU, *Anti-racism Charter*. Available online at: https://neu.org.uk/anti-racism-charter [accessed 5 September 2022].

15. See *SWLondoner*, 22 January 2021, 'Remote learning packages distributed to support Croydon students'. Available online at: www.swlondoner.co.uk/news/22012021-remote-learning-packages-croydon [accessed 5 September 2022].

16. See Society of Editors, 28 January 2021, 'Daily Mirror launches £1m "Help a Child to Learn" campaign for pens and books'. Available online at: www.societyofeditors.org/soe_news/daily-mirror-launches-1m-help-a-child-to-learn-campaign-for-pens-and-books/ [accessed 5 September 2022].

17. At its annual conference in April 2021, the union presented Marcus Rashford with the prestigious Fred and Anne Jarvis Award to recognise his contribution to successful campaigns to ensure school children continued to access their free school meals through holiday periods.

18. See *The Guardian*, 19 August 2021, '"Laughing stock": what the papers say about Gavin Williamson'. Available online at: www.theguardian.com/media/2020/aug/19/laughing-stock-what-papers-say-about-gavin-williamson-education-secretary-exams-front-pages [accessed 5 September 2022].

19. See *Mr Finch's blog*, 'NEU Celebrating Education conference'. Available online at: https://mrefinch.wordpress.com/2019/03/ [accessed 5 September 2022].

20. Here, we are using the term 'intellectual' to describe activists who engage others in the intellectual activity of debate and critical thinking. We are not referring to activists as 'intellectuals' in the more traditional sense.
21. Personal correspondence with one of the authors.
22. From NUT reps' training materials.

CHAPTER 7

1. Matt Luskin, 'Lessons of the Chicago teachers strike'. Available online at: www.youtube.com/watch?v=FZOTp_vZ-80 [accessed 5 September 2022].
2. 'Laura Pidcock's speech @ The Big Meeting, Durham Gala 2019'. Available online at: www.youtube.com/watch?v=LROFMOQGY3A [accessed 5 September 2022].
3. *StrikeMap* is an initiative to help build solidarity with workers taking industrial action by using web technologies to publicise disputes and encourage trade unionists to demonstrate practical support. See www.strikemap.co.uk.

References

All London Teachers Against Racism and Fascism 1984. *Challenging Racism*. London: ALTARF.

Ball, S. J. 1988. Staff relations during the teachers' industrial action: context, conflict and proletarianization. *British Journal of Sociology of Education*, 9(3), 289–306.

Ball, S. J. 2013. *The Education Debate* (2nd edn). Bristol, UK: Policy Press.

Becker, G. S. 1962. Investment in human capital: a theoretical analysis. *Journal of Political Economy*, 70(5), 9–49.

Bhattacharyya, G. 2018. *Rethinking Racial Capitalism: Questions of Reproduction and Survival*. London: Rowman & Littlefield.

Blanc, E. 2019. *Red State Revolt: The Teachers' Strikes and Working Class Politics*. London: Verso.

Carter, B. and Kline, R. 2017. The crisis of public sector trade unionism: evidence from the Mid Staffordshire Hospital crisis. *Capital & Class*, 41(2), 217–237.

Carter, B., Stevenson, H. and Passy, R. 2010. *Industrial Relations in Education: Transforming the School Workforce*. London: Routledge.

Casey, L. 2020. *The Teacher Insurgency: A Strategic and Organizing Perspective*. Cambridge, MA: Harvard University Press.

Chitty, C. 1993. 'Great Debate' or great betrayal? *Education Today and Tomorrow*, Spring, 9–10.

Compton, M. and Weiner, L. (eds) 2008. *The Global Assault on Teaching, Teachers and their Unions: Stories for Resistance*. New York: Palgrave Macmillan.

Connell, R. 1985. *Teachers' Work*. London: Routledge.

Courtney, K. and Little, G. 2014. Standing up for education: building a national campaign. *FORUM*, 56(2), 299–317.

Cox, C. B. and Dyson, A. E. (eds) 1969. *The Fight for Education: A Black Paper*. London: The Critical Quarterly Society.

D'Atri, A. 2022. *Bread and Roses: Gender and Class under Capitalism*. London: Left Book Club.

Davis, M. 2020. *Women and Class*. London: Manifesto.

de Turbeville, S. 2004. Does the 'organising model' represent a credible union renewal strategy? *Work, Employment and Society*, 18(4), 775–794.

Ellis, T., McWhirter, J., McColgan, D. and Haddow, B. 1976. *William Tyndale: The Teachers' Story*. London: Writers' and Readers' Publishing Co-operative.

Edmonds, J. and Tuffin, A. 1990. *A New Agenda: Bargaining for Prosperity in the 1990s*. London: General Municipal and Boilermakers' Union and Union of Communication Workers.

Fairbrother, P. 1984. *All Those in Favour: The Politics of Union Democracy.* London: Pluto Press.

Fairbrother, P. 1996. 'Workplace trade unionism in the state sector', in P. Ackers, C. Smith and P. Smith (eds), *The New Workplace and Trade Unionism: Critical Perspectives on Work and Organization.* London: Routledge, pp. 110–148.

Fantasia, R. 1988. *Cultures of Solidarity: Consciousness, Action and Contemporary American Workers.* Berkeley, CA: University of California Press.

Flanders, A. 1970. *Management and Unions: The Theory and Reform of Industrial Relations.* London: Faber.

Fletcher, B. and Gapasin, F. 2008. *Solidarity Divided: The Crisis in Organized Labor and a New Path to Social Justice.* Berkeley, CA: University of California Press.

Freire, P. 1970. *Pedagogy of the Oppressed.* London: Penguin.

Ganz, M. 2009. *Why David Sometimes Wins: Leadership, Organization and Strategy in the California Farm Worker Movement.* Oxford, UK: Oxford University Press.

Ganz, M. 2010. 'Leading change: leadership, organization and social movements', in N. Nohria and R. Khurana (eds), *Handbook of Leadership of Theory and Practice.* Boston, MA: Harvard Business Publishing, pp. 527–568.

Golin, S. 2002. *The Newark Teacher Strikes.* New Brunswick, NJ: Rutgers University Press.

Goodrich, C. L. 1920/1975. *The Frontier of Control: A Study in British Workshop Politics.* London: Pluto Press.

Gramsci, A. 1971. *Selections from the Prison Notebooks.* London: Lawrence & Wishart.

Han, H. 2014. *How Organizations Develop Activists: Civic Associations and Leadership in the 21st Century.* Oxford, UK: Oxford University Press.

Harvey, D. 2007. *A Brief History of Neoliberalism.* Oxford, UK: Oxford University Press.

Hayek, F. A. 1944/2001. *The Road to Serfdom.* London: Routledge.

Heery, E. 2002. Partnership versus organising: alternative futures for British trade unions. *Industrial Relations Journal*, 33(1), 20–35.

Hirsch, E. D. 1999. *The Schools We Need: And Why We Don't Have Them.* New York: Anchor Books.

Holgate, J. 2021. *Arise: Power, Strategy and Union Resurgence.* London: Pluto Press.

Jones, K. 2016. *Education in Britain: 1944 to the Present* (2nd edn). Cambridge, UK: Polity Press.

Kelly, J. 1996. 'Union militancy and social partnership', in P. Ackers, C. Smith and P. Smith (eds), *The New Workplace and Trade Unionism: Critical Perspectives on Work and Organization.* London: Routledge, pp. 77–109.

Kelly, J. 1998. *Rethinking Industrial Relations: Mobilisation, Collectivism and Long Waves.* London: Routledge.

Little, G. (ed.) 2015. *Global Education 'Reform': Building Resistance and Solidarity.* London: Manifesto Press.

Little, G. 2016. Global education reform and union responses. *Theory & Struggle*, 117, 134–150.

Little, G. and McDowell. L. 2017. 'Responding to social movement trade unionism within education', in M. Seal (ed.), *Trade Union Education: Transforming the World*. London: New Internationalist, pp. 185–201.

Lowe, R. 2007. *The Death of Progressive Education: How Teachers Lost Control of the Classroom*. London: Routledge.

Malm, A. 2020. *The Progress of This Storm: Nature and Society in a Warming World*. London: Verso.

Marks, R., Cox, S. and Little, G. 2022. Pockets of resistance: taking back control from within our education systems. *FORUM*, 64(2), 4–10.

McAlevey, J. 2016. *No Shortcuts: Organizing for Power in the New Gilded Age*. Oxford, UK: Oxford University Press.

McAlevey, J. 2020. *A Collective Bargain: Unions, Organizing, and the Fight for Democracy*. New York: Ecco.

McCarthy, W. E. J. 1966. *The Role of the Shop Steward in British Industrial Relations: Research Paper No. 1, Royal Commission on Trade Unions and Employers Associations*. London: HMSO.

Moody, K. 2020. Reversing the 'model': thoughts on Jane McAlevey's plans for union power. *Spectre*, 1(2), 61–75.

Muna, S., 2017. Partners in protest: parents, unions and anti-academy campaigns. *Industrial Relations Journal*, 48(4), 326–344.

Murphy, J. 1934/1972. *Preparing for Power: A Critical Study of the History of the British Working Class Movement*. London: Pluto Press.

Reay, D. 2017. *Miseducation: Inequality, Education and the Working Classes*. Bristol, UK: Policy Press.

Renton, D. 2014. The killing of Blair Peach. *London Review of Books*, 36(10), 23–26.

Richardson, B. (ed.) 2005. *Tell It Like It Is: How Our Schools Fail Black Children*. London: Bookmarks.

Rieser, R. 2016. The teachers' action, 1984–1986: learning lessons from history. *FORUM*, 58(2), 267–274.

Roediger, D. 2017. *Class, Race and Marxism*. London: Verso.

Seifert, R. 1987. *Teacher Militancy: A History of Teacher Strikes*. London: Falmer Press.

Seifert, R. and Sibley, T. 2012. *Revolutionary Communist at Work: A Political Biography of Bert Ramelson*. London: Lawrence & Wishart.

Simms, M. 2007. Managed activism: two union organising campaigns in the not-for-profit sector. *Industrial Relations Journal*, 38(2), 119–135.

Simon, B. 1984. Breaking school rules. *Marxism Today*, September, 19–25.

Simon, B. 1991. *Education and the Social Order 1940–1990*. London: Lawrence & Wishart.

Stevenson, H. 2001. 'Shifting Frontiers: Trade Union Responses to Changes in the Labour Process of Teaching'. Unpublished PhD thesis, Keele University.

Stevenson, H. 2005. From 'school correspondent' to workplace bargainer? The changing role of the school union representative. *British Journal of Sociology of Education*, 26(2), 219–233.

Stevenson, H. 2016. Challenging school reform from below: is leadership the missing link in mobilization theory? *Leadership and Policy in Schools*, 15(1), 67–90.

Stevenson, H. 2023. *Antonio Gramsci and Educational Leadership*. London: Routledge.

Stevenson, H., Carter, B., Milner, A. and Vega Castillo, M. 2020. *Your Turn: Teachers for Trade Union Renewal*. Brussels, Belgium: European Trade Union Committee for Education.

Tattersall, A. 2010. *Power in Coalition: Strategies for Strong Unions and Social Change*. Ithaca, NY: Cornell University Press.

Taylor, F. W. 1911/2004. *Scientific Management*. London: Routledge.

Undy, R. 2008. *Trade Union Merger Strategies: Purpose, Process, and Performance*. Oxford, UK: Oxford University Press.

Vygotsky, I. S. 1978. *Mind in Society: The Development of Higher Psychological Processes*. Cambridge, MA: Harvard University Press.

Weiner, L. 2012. *The Future of Our Schools: Teachers, Unions and Social Justice*. Chicago, IL: Haymarket Books.

Williams, R. 1989. *Resources of Hope*. London: Verso.

Winchip. E. 2022. Open for business: a quantitative analysis of teachers' experiences of marketisation in international schools, *Educational Review*. DOI: 10.1080/00131911.2022.2094343.

Index

fig refers to a figure; *n* to a note

Thanks to our Patreon subscriber:

Ciaran Kane

Who has shown generosity and comradeship in support of our publishing.

Check out the other perks you get by subscribing to our Patreon – visit patreon.com/plutopress.

Subscriptions start from £3 a month.